ONLY GOD

ONLY GOD
Transforming One Inmate and Family at a Time

Copyright © 2024 Mike Broyles

ISBN: 978-1-956220-80-3

Note: All Scriptures are taken from NIV except where otherwise noted.

Scriptures taken from the Holy Bible, New International Version®, NIV®. Copyright © 1973, 1978, 1984, 2011 by Biblica, Inc.™ Used by permission of Zondervan. All rights reserved worldwide.www.zondervan.comThe "NIV" and "New International Version" are trademarks registered in the United States Patent and Trademark Office by Biblica, Inc.™ Scripture quotations marked HCSB are taken from the Holman Christian Standard Bible®, Copyright © 1999, 2000, 2002, 2003, 2009 by Holman Bible Publishers. Used by permission. Holman Christian Standard Bible®, Holman CSB®, and HCSB® are federally registered trademarks of Holman Bible Publishers.

The names of some people have been changed or omitted to protect the privacy of those who have been or are still incarcerated. Any similarities to anyone by the names of inmates used in this book are unintentional and purely coincidental.

All rights reserved. No portion of this book may be reproduced mechanically, electronically, or by any other means, including photocopying, without the written permission of the author. It is illegal to copy the book, post it to a website, or distribute it by any other means without permission from the author.

Expert Press
www.ExpertPress.net

Expert Press
2 Shepard Hills Court
Little Rock, AR 72223
www.ExpertPress.net

Editing by Valerie Riese
Copyediting by Lori Price
Proofreading by Heather Dubnick
Text design and composition by Emily Fritz
Cover design by Casey Fritz
Front cover photographer by Jeff Steele

ONLY GOD

TRANSFORMING ONE INMATE AND FAMILY AT A TIME

MIKE BROYLES

CONTENTS

DEDICATION		i
ACKNOWLEDGMENTS		iii
FOREWORD		1
1	FROM FEAR TO FAITH	5
2	ENTERING THE BLOODIEST PRISON IN AMERICA: LOUISIANA STATE PENITENTIARY	15
3	MIRACLES AT L.A. COUNTY JAIL	23
4	TOOLS FOR IMPACTING FAMILIES	33
5	BUILDING HEALTHY FAMILIES FROM INSIDE PRISON	43
6	WHAT I HAVE LEARNED FROM THE INMATES	57
7	WHAT I HAVE LEARNED FROM PRISON LEADERS	67
8	INTERNATIONAL PRISONS . . . GO	81
9	HOW CHURCHES CAN GET INVOLVED IN PRISON MINISTRY	93
10	FINISHING WELL	103
11	A NEW MODEL FOR PRISONS	111
KEY BIBLE VERSES FOR THE INMATE IN ALL OF US		119
PRAYER OF SALVATION		121
LIFELINE GLOBAL CURRICULUM		123
ABOUT THE AUTHOR		125

DEDICATION

First and foremost, this book is about giving God the glory for transforming one life and one family at a time through the power of the resurrection of Christ. Only God!

"And without faith it is impossible to please God, because anyone who comes to him must believe that he exists and that he rewards those who earnestly seek him" (Hebrews 11:6).

This material is dedicated to my family. Thank you for putting up with all my prison stories and time away traveling for the ministry. I could never express enough gratitude to my sweetheart and wife, Debbie. Thank you for your prayers, care, crying, and laughing together through over fifty-two years of marriage and in these crazy good days of prison ministry. You're my gift from God. I never could have done this without your support.

And to my kids and their families, who are living out the gospel of Christ every day in different ways and places all over the world. Thank you to my sons, Dan and Jon, my daughters-in-law, Carli and Jocelyn, and my grandchildren, Emma, Nate, Josiah, Nolan, Lucas, Eli, and Saffron.

Especially to my grandkids, I dedicate this book to you so Christ will use each of you to impact your world with the good news of Christ. That's my prayer for each of you!

"Jesus replied, 'Love the Lord your God with all your heart and with all your soul and with all your mind. This is the first and greatest commandment. And the second is like it: 'Love your neighbor as yourself'" (Matthew 22:37–39).

Lastly, I dedicate this book to all the inmates who have taken classes in Malachi Dads or Hannah's Gift, praying that God will use you in turning your children, grandchildren, community, and the world toward Jesus Christ! Like me, you have experienced the grace and forgiveness of Christ. Now, let's step up the pace to see our world transformed by the good news of Christ. Thank you for teaching me how to follow Christ!

ONLY GOD!

ACKNOWLEDGMENTS

This book would not have been possible without key people whom God used to lay a foundation to impact my life for the gospel through Lifeline Global Ministries, especially in our early days.

The Awana Clubs International leadership team of Lyndon Azcuna, Brian Rhodes, Art Rorheim, and Jack Eggar, who helped birth Lifeline Global Ministries, stepped out of the box of Awana Clubs with a vision of reaching kids and their fathers and mothers for Christ along with the help of Warden Burl Cain.

I have had the delight of working with the Lifeline Global staff, who, by faith and with great support, have been the hands and feet that Christ used to reach and touch thousands of inmates and their kids. They are the true heroes of our ministry. Our Lifeline Global president and leader, Dr. Rumney Ruder, not only teaches Malachi Dads but keeps us going steady with his gifts of administration and follow-through for the business side of ministry.

Along with our staff are thousands of volunteers and donors who cared and taught God's Word by stepping out of their comfort zone to go into prisons and jails all over the world. And to those who have generously given to prison ministry, a big "thank you" for your faith steps that, as of this writing, have allowed us to be in thirty-three states across the USA and twenty countries around the world.

Also, I want to give a big "shout out" to my mentors in prison ministries because I really needed you to show me the way to work in jails and prisons. I have been a pastor for years with no background in prison policy and yet you coached me each step of the way as I learned about "prison culture." Thank you for your leadership, example, care, and willingness to listen. Thank you, David Bates, Alex Yim, and Burl Cain. I learned from the best. I also send a thank you to my dear friend who now enjoys heaven, Joe Feinstein. Joe was my son's father-in-law and my own brother in Christ. Thank you for helping me in this life-changing ministry with inmates and their families. Thanks for your quiet faithfulness in teaching inmates to follow Christ and cheering me along as we started this crazy family ministry to broken families on the inside. You are missed but never forgotten.

And lastly, this book would never have been done without Valerie Riese's encouragement, direction, skill, and patience with the process. Thank you for believing in me that we could finish this book. Thank you.

FOREWORD

Mike Broyles's book *Only God: Transforming One Inmate and Family at a Time* is a great example of transformation originating in the most unlikely place, the Louisiana State Penitentiary at Angola. When I told Awana Founder Art Rorheim that prisoners' children are seven times more likely than other children to go to prison, he sent Awana CEO Jack Eggar and staffer Lyndon Azcuna to Angola to minister to the inmates and find a way to minister to the prisoners' children.

During one of their visits, Lyndon and I began a five-minute drive from the main prison to the ranch house when he told me he needed an hour to explain a children's program Awana wanted to introduce to the prisoners. I told him, "Tell me now; it doesn't take an hour for me to make a decision." By the time we arrived at the ranch house, I knew the idea was a winner.

When we introduced the program to the inmate ministers and prison church leaders, we tasked them with naming the program. They chose "Malachi Dads" to remember the biblical Malachi, who told fathers to care for their children.

The author of this book, Mike Broyles, came on board with Awana to develop the *Malachi Dads* program and expand it to other states. The *Malachi Dads* curriculum now ministers to children across the United States and many other countries.

Mike realized we had to do something for the female inmates' children, so he, Angola Chaplain Jim Rentz, and I launched a parallel to the *Malachi Dads* program called *"Hannah's Gift."*

Mike Broyles's book leads the reader on a journey of God's grace and love for children. You will see the miracle of a wonderful program birthed in the most unlikely place—a prison—just as Joseph was in prison when God opened the door for His chosen. Our God still today uses unlikely places to perform His miracles. This book is an inspiration and a blessing to readers.

—BURL CAIN
Commissioner of the Mississippi Department of Corrections and former warden at the Louisiana State Penitentiary at Angola

PART 1
THE STORY OF LIFELINE GLOBAL

1
FROM FEAR TO FAITH

When I am afraid, I put my trust in you.
—PSALM 56:3

I grew up in Southern California in what was considered a typical family. My dad was a chef. My mother expressed her creativity as a floral artist. My only sibling is a brother seven years older, so I grew up as an only child.

I'm thankful for a childhood where I was loved and cared for by Christian parents. My earliest memories include going to church, praying as a family, and talking about spiritual things.

My greatest fear was speaking in front of people, so I was a reserved kid with just a few friends. But I loved baseball. I was an excellent pitcher, and baseball helped me overcome my shyness. My world revolved around baseball. In fact, by the time I was twelve or thirteen years old, baseball was like my god rather than a hobby.

I was an average student overall, but I struggled in English class because the idea of speaking in front of my peers made me sick with fear. I refused to even try to speak in front of people, so I failed English three times in a row my sophomore year. At the same time I struggled in school, I suddenly lost the physical ability to pitch baseball. Overnight, I went from being a star pitcher to being unable to throw the ball. I just felt awkward physically. So when I lost baseball, I also lost interest in school.

It seemed no one sensed how discouraged I was between baseball and academics. Even when I felt like giving up, my teachers still knew me as a good kid. In the fall of my senior year, the school counselor awarded me Citizen of the Year for my small community. I went to a fancy dinner to receive my award, and a week later, I dropped out of school.

The day I dropped out, I only thought of myself, but my perspective changed when I faced my parents. They didn't have the opportunity to go to school past eighth grade, and they worked hard so I could get an education. My parents were loving and patient, and my decision especially hurt my mom. Their disappointment changed how I saw myself.

Since I wasn't in school, it was time to get a job. At age seventeen, I entered the workforce full time as a dishwasher at the senior center, where my dad was the head chef. After about two years of mopping the floors and scrubbing pots and pans, I realized I needed to make a better wage.

My uncle helped me get the most wonderfully boring job at a factory that made vacuum cleaners. I sat in a chair and pulled a lever down to put together a small part for each vacuum cleaner. Then, I put the part in a box. For eight hours every day, I would sit there, pull the lever, box the part, pull the lever, box the part, until the boredom became unbearable.

There was no way I could do this for the rest of my life, so I decided to go back to school.

My second year at the factory, I enrolled in night school, where the same nauseating fears greeted me at the door. My first class was psychology, with about twenty other students. Just before the evening break, the teacher said that when we returned, every student would walk to the front of the class to introduce themselves.

I raced for the door, into the hallway, and through the crowd to a secluded corner where the intersection to my future waited. I leaned against the wall for support, hung my head, and whispered, "I don't need this, Lord. I can't do this; I don't know how!"

As I pleaded to God both for my future and for my lunch to stay down, I noticed a red glow on the floor. My gaze followed it down the hall where the glow became brighter until I looked up to see the exit sign announcing my way of escape.

At that moment, I thought of my parents. Suddenly, I was overcome by an emotion even worse than fear—emptiness.

"Please help me, Lord," I prayed. "I can't do this without You."

I would love to tell you about how I was showered with peace and strength at that very moment. I could describe how I broadened my shoulders, marched back to class, and stood in front, waiting to open student introductions. But that would be a lie. Honestly, I don't remember how I did it, but somehow, the Lord helped me do the right thing. It was not my own fortitude but the grace of God that got me through that night and every night after.

The next year was very busy, and I grew both academically and spiritually. God used my high school youth sponsors, Gary and Diane Strickler, to support me. I worked in the factory every weekday, went to school four nights per week, and went to Bible study at the Stricklers' every Monday between work and school. The Stricklers not only taught the Bible, they lived it.

Diane was a great cook, and she knew I loved pumpkin pie, so she made a pie for me every Monday night to make sure I'd come. Gary became like a mentor to me during those Monday night Bible studies. He took the time to pray with me and held me accountable for my schoolwork.

Monday nights were also an opportunity to get to know other young adults who were stronger believers than I was. They were my support group.

Gary, Diane, and my friends cheered me on. When I finished my diploma, we all joined my parents and went out to dinner to celebrate. The meal ended with Diane's homemade pumpkin pie for dessert.

I got my diploma in 1968, but my public speaking days were far from over. Early in 1969, my church asked me to chaperone a vacation Bible school with about forty school-age kids from a small community in northern California. When we got there, I learned I would have to teach a twenty-minute session.

I chose to obey God rather than resist, so I prayed, I studied, and I prepared.

My session was just before lunch. The rest of the camp staff planned to prepare lunch in the kitchen just behind me as I began the twenty-minute lesson. Nearly forty kids sat before me, waiting for the day's pre-lunch food for thought. Less than four minutes later, I was done. My stunned colleagues scrambled to get the food ready as the kids began forming a line for lunch.

It may have been the shortest presentation in vacation Bible school history, but for me, it was both a simple and significant step of obedience to the Lord.

I started dating my wife that spring. Debbie and I grew up in the same church where our fathers were elders. Life was good until about three months later when I received a welcome letter from the United States Army.

I was assigned to infantry training, which meant I was headed for combat at the front lines in the Vietnam War in the summer of 1969. Debbie and I knew I might not make it back, but we promised to pray and write every day.

After basic training, I was assigned to a battalion of about one thousand men whose brothers were killed or seriously wounded in Vietnam. To protect the families from multiple losses, the battalion would never see live combat. Whether it was a mistake or the graciousness of the Lord, I don't know, but I was the only soldier in the battalion without a wounded brother.

The battalion spent the next year on standby at Fort Campbell, Kentucky. We did military drills, practiced shooting, rode in helicopters and tanks, and perfected maneuvers. I also spent the year learning from one of the greatest leaders I have ever met.

My sergeant had been to Vietnam three times. He was shot during his third tour, so the government did not send him back into combat. Sergeant just knew how to lead and motivate men. He knew how to be hard and how to be tender. He led by example. The night before inspections, he didn't just tell us to clean the barracks. He got down on his hands and knees and scrubbed the floors with us. Whatever yucky thing we had to do, he was doing it first every week.

I grew both as a man and as a spiritual leader thanks to Sergeant. I lived with about thirty other young men. We did everything together, so we knew each other's struggles. Many men grappled with depression, fear, alcohol, and thoughts of suicide. Although I had no seminary training, the men called me "Reverend" because Sergeant called on me to counsel them, often in the middle of the night. Sergeant was a tremendous encouragement because he believed in me.

During my year at Fort Campbell, I discovered "Christian Servicemen," a family-run outreach ministry for military men living far from home. They had an apartment with a pool table, ping-pong tables, games, homemade cookies, and beds for the men to stay overnight. When the soldiers came into town on the weekends, they would see signs advertising free food, games, and fun, so the center was always busy.

An outstanding, Christ-honoring family ran the ministry. I spent weekends with them so I could minister to the men, and they became like family to me. They took me in as one of their own and loved on me like a son.

The time I spent at Christian Servicemen was life-changing. Many of the men knew they were going to Vietnam soon, so they were open to spiritual conversations. We would share about the love of God and how Christ could save them from their sins. I was able to lead soldiers to Jesus every week for a year. That's when I sensed God calling me to be a pastor and spiritual leader.

In 1970, our battalion moved to the German border to guard nuclear missiles. Germany, Switzerland, and Austria were beautiful. I continued to overcome my fear of public speaking as the chaplain encouraged me to read Scripture and pray publicly.

My relationship with Debbie grew through letters while I was in Fort Campbell. During a brief leave in 1970, we knew it was getting serious, so we agreed to write letters daily after I went back to the army and she returned to college in Canada.

But when I got to Germany, the letters stopped. For a month, I wrote to her every day and heard nothing from my Debbie, all while my buddies around me opened "Dear John" letters. Just as doubt set in, Debbie realized she had my address wrong. The day I received thirty letters was one of the greatest days of my life!

I got out of the army early in 1971 and continued to write to her every day until she came home to California that summer. I asked my Debbie to marry me on Memorial Day. She said yes, and we spent the next few weeks trying to figure out what to do about our future.

I wanted to go to a Bible college, but school was difficult for me. I found a small Christian school in Omaha, Nebraska, where I could use my veteran benefits. One Sunday afternoon in July, I told Debbie I couldn't wait for her to be my wife any longer. With our parents' blessing, in one short month, we planned a Friday-night wedding for eight hundred people, spent the weekend honeymooning in Malibu, packed everything we could in our Volkswagen Bug, and headed for Nebraska on Monday night.

We didn't know where we were going. We had no job, no place to live, and no friends waiting for us in Omaha. Somehow, on Friday afternoon, we made it to the college two hours before registration closed for the semester. I had to update my marital status to get out of the dorms, and Debbie had to transfer from her school in Canada. By the grace of God, we were both accepted to the college in the last hour.

Next, we had to find a place to live. The housing was so bad, my new bride was in tears until we learned the current resident of an apartment owned by the school was moving out in two days. The apartment was affordable and only a block from school.

In one crazy week, we got married, moved across the country, enrolled in college, and found our first apartment together. But the adventure wasn't over yet.

Next stop: speech class. A few years prior, a teacher like Mr. Penner was my greatest fear. But I was a different man now. I was a man of faith.

During every class period, each student had to do a different public speaking exercise. One day, I had to tell the story of the three bears. Another day, the class of twenty students booed and hissed while I spoke. One afternoon, the audience of my peers acted like drunks, out of control. And I survived every class.

Mr. Penner's speech class was transformational because he knew how to bring out the best in his students. He made us all better without putting us down. He gave me confidence to move from paralyzing fear to faith that God will always give me strength.

Jesus answered, "I am the way and the truth and the life. No one comes to the Father except through me."
—JOHN 14:6

2
ENTERING THE BLOODIEST PRISON IN AMERICA: LOUISIANA STATE PENITENTIARY

And he will turn the hearts of fathers to their children and the hearts of children to their fathers. Otherwise, I will come and strike the land with a curse.
—MALACHI 4:6 HCSB

In 2007, I was an associate pastor at Grace Baptist Church in Los Angeles, California. One day, I received an email from Awana Clubs International looking for people to help with a carnival organized by their prison ministry, Awana Lifeline. The email said the Returning Hearts Celebration was a carnival to help inmates reconcile with their children. They needed volunteers to help with carnival games at Louisiana State Penitentiary.

Being the wonderful pastor that I was, I sent two men from church to check it out. Joe Feinstein was a chaplain with the Los Angeles County jail system, so I asked him and another gentleman to go. They loved it, so they went back the next year and returned determined to get me involved. In over forty years as a pastor, I had never even visited a prison. I thought they were nuts to involve me, but they persisted.

I agreed to serve at L.A. County Jail as a prison chaplain, where I ministered to about 9,000 men throughout four local jails. In 2009, that meant leading church service inside the jails, talking and praying with the men, and helping them become more godly men for themselves, their families, and their communities.

As God changed my heart toward the inmates, Joe became friends with Deputy Sheriff David Bates. Joe shared videos of a Returning Hearts Celebration and other things he learned about the culture during his two visits to Angola. David was a Christian, so he soaked up everything Joe told him about the attitudes of the inmates and Warden Cain.

When Joe introduced me to David, we formed a team to discuss how to better minister to the men and women at L.A. County Jail. Before I knew it, I was on a plane to New Orleans.

Louisiana State Penitentiary, also known as Angola, has a long, challenging history of violence, death, and hopelessness. Angola is a maximum-security prison for inmates with a life sentence of at least twenty years. In 2009, the average sentence for inmates in Angola was ninety-three years. Through the 1960s and 1970s, Angola was known as the "Bloodiest Prison in America" because of daily stabbings between inmates and between inmates and officers.

My flight from Los Angeles, California, landed in New Orleans at about 10:00 p.m., but my travel adventure was just beginning. I still had another two-hour drive to Angola.

Raindrops fell as I left New Orleans, and streetlights were in the rear-view mirror. I was a city boy headed for southern farmland, so I had to get there before the rain got much worse.

An hour later, as I splashed through the mud and past another field, I strained through the pouring rain to catch a glimpse of civilization. I thanked God I didn't blink and miss the entire town of St. Francisville and the chance to get directions. Sadly, no one seemed too willing to talk about Angola.

I continued the journey, longing to trade the beauty of the farmland for the familiarity of freeways. When I realized I couldn't remember the last time I had seen oncoming traffic, I prayed I wouldn't drive off the end of the earth, never to be heard from again.

I reached the front gate of the "Alcatraz of the South" around midnight. The guard checked me in and gave me a map with directions to the dorm where I would be staying. Much to my dismay, it wasn't a map of how to get around a building. The map depicted 18,000 acres of prison farmland, with five large rectangles representing each of the separate prisons, all accessible by twenty miles of dirt roads. The guard circled the Training Center, where I would bunk for the night, and sent me on my way.

I prayed through the dark, flooded campus while the mud sucked me into a ditch twice by the time I found the Training Center, located right next to death row. Uncertain if I was truly glad I had reached my destination, I grabbed my bag and dodged the pelting raindrops until I got to the door. A guard let me in and pointed down the hall to the dorm.

I stood in the doorway for a moment. The clock on the other side of the room said 1:00 a.m. I counted twenty beds, half of which were already occupied by sleeping men. I was too tired to care. I found an empty bed and fell fast asleep, trusting God knew what I would discover in the morning.

My visit to Louisiana State Penitentiary in 2009 was about halfway through Burl Cain's transformative tenure as warden. Thanks to the power of the gospel as implemented by Warden Cain, my first experience in prison ministry was at the safest, most secure prison in America.

When Mr. Cain became the very hesitant warden of Angola in 1995, one of the first things he did was partner with New Orleans Baptist Theological Seminary (NOBTS). In 1996, professors from the seminary paid for their own travel, time, and materials to teach the prisoners "moral rehabilitation," where prisoners learn they are created in the image of God, and they are loved and forgiven by their Creator.

Daily stabbings at Angola became a thing of the past, along with gangs, fights, and even cursing. These staples of prison life were replaced by inmate pastors, churches, and prayers. The prison was no longer a financial anchor for the state. Instead, Angola was almost a self-sustaining city, including a fully functioning farm, a woodshop, and a hospice program established in 1997.

But I was there to learn about a carnival for the inmates' children. In 2004, several Christian inmates confided in Warden Cain their concerns for their children. The fathers didn't want their kids to make the same mistakes they did. They wanted a better future for their children, but they didn't know what they could do as prisoners serving a life sentence inside a maximum-security prison. Warden Cain didn't know how to answer their questions, but he promised to figure it out.

He started with Awana Clubs International in Chicago, a suburban ministry for children. Warden Cain formed a leadership team with five inmates and Awana leadership. The inmate leader of the team was especially passionate about bridging the separation between the inmate fathers and their children. Together, the men came up with an idea for a Bible study to help prisoners be better men and fathers, even from inside prison. The men who went through the Bible study program would then be eligible to attend the annual Returning Hearts Celebration.

Awana leadership believed it would be a tough sell, but they were willing to explore the idea. One of their executives scheduled two hours with Warden Burl Cain and flew down from Chicago to New Orleans. When they got to Angola, the Awana executive and Burl went for a drive to talk. Five minutes into the drive, Malachi Dads and Returning Hearts Celebration were born.

In 2004, Burl Cain and Awana leadership formed a business partnership they called Awana Lifeline, a ministry dedicated to inspiring and equipping incarcerated parents to be godly fathers and mothers. The main purpose was to give the inmates time to reconcile with their children, seek forgiveness, and begin to have a real parent and child relationship.

By 2009, Malachi Dads and the Returning Hearts Celebration had been transformational for many inmates at Angola and their families, thanks to inmates and the prison leaders who took the time to listen.

Now it was my turn.

Life without God is like an unsharpened pencil—it has no point.
—BILLY GRAHAM

3
MIRACLES AT L.A. COUNTY JAIL

Continue to remember those in prison as if you were together with them in prison, and those who are mistreated as if you yourselves were suffering.
—HEBREWS 13:3

When I returned home, Joe, Dave, and I started making plans to help inmates of L.A. County Jail reconcile with their children during a Returning Hearts Celebration.

Los Angeles (L.A.) County Jail is the largest jail system in America, consisting of eight detention centers, each with several jailhouse facilities. With such a large organization and enough bureaucracy to manage approximately 12,000 jobs and over 20,000 inmates, we knew starting a new ministry would be a challenge.

As expected, bureaucracy was thick and slow, but God gave us a wonderful contact within the L.A. County Jail's leadership who was second-in-command to the sheriff. Chief Alex Yim was a Christian and an outstanding police officer, a cop's cop who took pride in taking criminals off the streets, locking them up, and throwing away the key. Unfortunately, he wasn't a big believer in second chances, but his pastor son, Brent, was teaching his father to love people even in the midst of crime.

Chief Yim was willing to learn, so when we heard the next Returning Hearts Celebration was about to be held at Angola, Alex, Brent, David, and I decided to fly to Louisiana to see it for ourselves.

When we met with Warden Cain, he took us behind the scenes to discover how the inmates prepare for the Returning Hearts Celebration through the *Malachi Dads* Bible study. We were all overwhelmed by the attitudes of joy and contentment in the Malachi Dads leadership team. Criminals serving life sentences in a maximum-security prison for unimaginable acts stood before us as men transformed into spiritual leaders to their fellow inmates.

The father-son interaction between Alex and Brent during the visit was beautiful. As we got to know the Malachi Dads men, the Lord used Brent to soften his dad's heart. Alex began to see the inmates through fresh eyes, as men made in the image of God. Alex realized the men still had value despite the terrible crimes of their past.

We were all especially taken by Randy. Randy was a very young man when he was sentenced to life in prison in Angola. To protect himself and the other inmates, he spent his first year in solitary confinement. One day, Randy asked a guard for a Bible. He spent many hours reading the Bible every day, and he gave his heart to Christ in solitary confinement. Randy then joined the general population and grew into a spiritual leader for the men inside Angola.

We were so inspired by Randy's story that Dave asked Warden Cain for permission to have Randy join us for lunch. We wanted to get to know Randy away from the other inmates, so Warden Cain allowed Randy to meet us at the Ranch House, an area typically only used for guests.

Randy was known for his beautiful voice and guitar skills. Chief Yim was taken aback as Randy filled the Ranch House and our hearts with sincere praise and worship music. In fact, Alex was so struck by Randy's story that, with Warden Cain's permission, he gave Randy a new designer golf shirt he had purchased for the trip to Angola.

Brent, David, Alex, and I saw God's redemption during our visit to what had been known as the bloodiest prison in America. Through interactions with Randy and other Malachi Dads leaders, we all understood that the inmates inside Angola were still human beings, loved by God.

We got back to Los Angeles more determined than ever. At times, the bureaucracy of the largest jail system in the nation nearly pushed us into throwing in the towel. We did not know what we were doing, but we knew we couldn't do it alone. One day, I told Joe we should recruit fellow members from Grace Baptist Church to help. I wanted the best, most faithful people with the energy to make Returning Hearts a reality at the L.A. County Jail.

The Lord gave us twelve tenacious people who weren't afraid of the situation or hard work. We prayed, planned, and learned everything we could from the leaders in Angola. When another Returning Hearts Celebration was announced at a different prison outside Baton Rouge, two ladies from our group flew to Louisiana to gather all the knowledge and resources they could.

I continued serving as a chaplain for Pitchess Detention Center while our planning committee at Grace Baptist Church worked through the jail system bureaucracy. One Friday evening, I led a church service for about 180 inmates. After the sermon, one of the instructors told me seventy-five of the men wanted to come to faith.

Giving your life to Christ while in prison is risky, especially if it means forsaking your gang. I was shocked, and honestly, I didn't think they all knew what they were doing. I explained the risk and asked them three times if this was what they wanted. The men had made up their mind, and I was used by God for a revival that night.

The following Sunday night, Deputy Sheriff David Bates was with me at church when he got a call to report to the jail immediately because a riot had broken out in a different area of Pitchess Detention Center.

Officers worked hard to stop it, but the chaos gained momentum as it moved from one part of the detention center to the next. Eventually, the riot reached the cell block where, two nights prior, I had preached and God had led seventy-five men to faith. Instead of joining the violence, all seventy-five new believers—young and old, different races, and enemy gang affiliations—joined together in peace. The older men locked arms and prayed while the younger men protected them, and together, they stopped the riot.

As news of the riot spread, inmates and officers questioned how it suddenly stopped. During the investigation, Deputy Bates testified that in twenty-five years as a police officer, he had never seen inmates come together in peace. He knew the riots were stopped by the grace of God, a miracle through these new men in faith.

The courage of those men proved God is still working miracles in people we think are lost. As a result, my team was blessed with the respect we needed. After about eighteen months of planning and bureaucracy, my team got the sheriff's approval and the support of the department to move forward.

With our newfound credibility and freedom, David, Joe, and I were introduced to the captain of the L.A. Jail system. She was an amazing woman with a beautiful balance of tenderness and tenacity. With her support, we went into full-bore planning mode, and the response from the community was overwhelming.

The strangest thing I have done in fifty years as a pastor happened during a Returning Hearts volunteer orientation event at Grace Baptist Church. We needed about 250 volunteers willing to spend the day inside the L.A. County Jail with the inmates and their families. It was a big ask, but God was about to demonstrate His work in the hearts of the people at Grace Baptist Church.

People started to trickle in for the meeting, and they kept on coming until the seats were full and interested volunteers were standing at the back of the room. Over three hundred people showed up to volunteer for a fledgling jail ministry about which we had little information. It was the only time in my entire career as a pastor that I had to turn away so many volunteers.

Even after I fired eighty unpaid workers, God continued to be faithful. He provided five mature believers from Grace Baptist to write the *Malachi Dads* outline using information we brought back from Angola. All five men had strong Bible backgrounds, and two of them were skilled writers.

There were no Bible studies written specifically for inmates, so they borrowed Bible studies and curricula from other publishers. After the writers crafted the outline for the lesson each week, they gave a copy to the other men by Friday so they could all teach it Saturday morning.

Joe and Dave knew the men inside Pitchess Detention Center, so they worked with the captain to screen the inmates. Together, they chose the first twenty-five men to participate in the *Malachi Dads* Bible study and the Returning Hearts Celebration.

As the Bible studies began, other volunteers continued to prepare for the carnival. There are two goals for a Returning Hearts Celebration. It's more than a time for the men to make precious memories with their children; it's also an opportunity for restoration. Amid the fun of the day, parents have a chance to ask their children's forgiveness and to invite them to know the love and salvation available to them through accepting Christ as their Savior. A Returning Hearts Celebration can be the catalyst to heal a family and break not only the cycle of sin but also the intergenerational cycle of incarceration.

Another team of volunteers through Grace Baptist Church created a guardian program for the mothers, grandmothers, aunts, and uncles who would bring the children from all over L.A. County to see their dads at the carnival. We want the loved ones who step in to care for the children to know they are the real champions, so we sponsor a beautiful luncheon and give them special gifts.

There are countless details in planning any event, and even more when safety is a real concern, but the Lord protects us. We never had an issue during the first Returning Hearts Celebration or any other event worldwide since then.

Finally, the day for the first Returning Hearts Celebration at the L.A. County Jail arrived. Pitchess Detention Center was bursting with mixed emotions, including the officers on duty for the event. The deputies made their feelings known as they lined the perimeter, arms folded in disgust at the sight of children and volunteers inside the jail.

The *Malachi Dads* participants sat in rows at one end of the tent. Every man strained to see if his son or daughter was the next in line at the tent entrance. As each father and child were called by name, they ran to meet in a giant embrace in the middle of the field.

As I watched the children love on their daddies and the Malachi Dads hold their little ones tight, I noticed a change in the deputies surrounding the tent. As they saw the love all around, their arms relaxed, and there was not a dry eye in the tent.

For the first time, the officers saw the inmates as human beings, as men made in the image of God and loved by their Creator. About thirty minutes into the event, the captain approached me and said, "Can we do this next month? This is one of the most beautiful things I've ever seen."

The Malachi Dads ministry gained a lot of momentum after the first event. We held Returning Hearts celebrations in other L.A. County detention centers, and in two years, approximately four hundred men were baptized. It was all made possible by God's faithfulness through the volunteers, the officers, and the bravery of seventy-five new believers during that miracle at L.A. County Jail.

I want to stay in the habit of "glancing" at my problems and "gazing" at my Lord.
—JONI EARECKSON TADA

4
TOOLS FOR IMPACTING FAMILIES

For Ezra had devoted himself to the study and observance of the Law of the Lord, and to teaching its decrees and laws in Israel.
—EZRA 7:10

Two years later, the *Malachi Dads* Bible study was taught in Louisiana and five other states. We were still using the basic outline written for the first Returning Hearts Celebration in 2009, so my first mission as executive director in 2011 was to develop a coordinated curriculum to expand our impact and help inmates reconcile with their families.

I gave the outlines written by the original volunteers of Grace Baptist Church to a professional writer who wrote the first book called, *Malachi Dads: The Heart of a Father*. It is a Christ-honoring Bible study that focuses on how to be a godly man, husband, and father. We were off to a great start, and I was very pleased.

Once again, the Lord blessed our ministry with amazing people. I was friends with the founder of the National Center for Fathering, Dr. Ken Canfield. During lunch one day, I took notes while we brainstormed ideas for a curriculum consisting of four books.

The president of Awana Clubs International was friends with Dr. Gene Getz, author of the classic book *Measure of a Man: Twenty Attributes of a Godly Man*. He asked Dr. Getz to write *Malachi Dads: The Heart of a Man*, parts one and two, based on *Measure of a Man*, but with a special focus on character and integrity.

Our partnerships with Ken and Gene were a blessing because their contributions gave Lifeline additional credibility. Lifeline Global Ministries finally had our first curriculum. To this day, I am very proud of the writers and everyone who contributed.

My next mission was to minister to the female inmates. I was friends with Dr. Kristi Miller Anderson. Dr. Miller Anderson earned a PhD from NOBTS. She remained at NOBTS as a chaplain and started a women's seminary inside the Louisiana Correctional Institute for Women. I was thrilled when she agreed to write the parallel book to *Malachi Dads: The Heart of a Father*. She started by writing outlines and teaching them to the women enrolled in her seminary program. The women loved it, so she put it together in a book we called *Hannah's Gift: The Heart of a Mother*.

Kristi is an amazing author and teacher. The female inmates loved *Hannah's Gift*, and both Warden Cain and I were very impressed. It was a win for everyone, so I continued working with Kristi to build out the women's curriculum.

Next, Kristi wrote *Hannah's Gift: Family Restoration* based on the book of Jeremiah. The book was so good that we hired an editor to put it in masculine terms, and we added *Malachi Dads: Family Restoration* to the men's curriculum.

Then, Kristi wrote a wonderful book called *Hannah's Gift: Beautiful Woman* to help women learn about what it means to be beautiful in God's eyes. When we finished, the curriculum consisted of four books for the men and three for the women, all taught in small groups inside prison. Until 2020...

As it did every other organization in the world, the COVID pandemic forced us to think differently about how we do business. My team and I sought the Lord to determine how we could minister to the inmates when they couldn't get out and we couldn't go in.

We knew we had to put the curriculum on video, but we did not have the knowledge, skill set, or nearly $8,000 to do it effectively. As always, the Lord provided amazing people to help. One day, I told a good friend that we were trying to put *Malachi Dads* and *Hannah's Gift* on video, and he just took out his checkbook and wrote me a check for $7,500.

My next call was to Gary and Cindy Hall. Gary was a retired executive from Fox Network who started the Hollywood Impact ministry to give inmates an employable skill when they got out. With equipment generously donated by Fox, Gary and Cindy went inside jails and prisons, including Angola Prison and L.A. County Jail, to teach courses about photo shoots, lighting, recording, and videotaping.

Gary and Cindy were happy to videotape our *Malachi Dads* curriculum at Grace Baptist Church for no charge. When we finished, I asked him how much a project like this would cost. He told me most professionals would charge around $7,000, so I gladly gave him a nice donation toward his ministry.

The greatest joy of the project was working with one of Gary's cameramen, a former *Malachi Dads* graduate from Pitchess Detention Center. He had been in and out of prison for over twenty years by the time he enrolled in Malachi Dads in hopes of restoring the broken relationship with his daughter. One morning before we began shooting, he called his daughter, who was expecting a child soon. That man now has a healthy relationship with both his daughter and his baby granddaughter.

The videotapes for the rest of our curricula were done by the graciousness and generosity of our author friend, Dr. Gene Getz. He gave us use of his studio, recording equipment, and cameraman, so we gave a donation to his ministry, Renewal Ministries.

Malachi Dads and *Hannah's Gift* were now available on DVD for anyone who wanted it, but I was determined to get it to everyone who needed it, especially during COVID lockdowns. Early in the process of filming, I called a friend who worked in the prison system helping inmates get their GED. I knew parenting was important to him, so I told him we were putting our curricula on DVD. Immediately, he connected me with the prison television network. Now, *Hannah's Gift* and *Malachi Dads* are on the prison television network every day at 4 a.m. and 4 p.m. in the state of California.

Crime and incarceration are a generational curse. Statistics vary, but most studies report that over 70 percent of inmates had an incarcerated parent and that a child who has an incarcerated parent is as much as three times more likely to wind up in jail.

After serving with Lifeline Global for fifteen years, I am convinced that crime follows from generation to generation. I have met only one male inmate who said he had a good father at home. Most of the male inmates were either abused or abandoned by their fathers.

The Lifeline Global Bible curriculum is the only collection of Bible studies written specifically for the broken inmate—mom or dad—to help restore families and break the generational cycle of incarceration. Statistics also show that after five years behind bars, the only visitors most inmates see are their mothers. All others have given up.

That's why we believe restoration must begin the first day the parent spends behind bars, not the last. Our curriculum is designed to teach inmates how they can seek forgiveness and be restored with their children while they're still in prison, rather than waiting to be released.

Most of our Bible studies take place during a small group setting lasting two hours for ten–twelve weeks. Lessons consist of reading, curriculum work, discussion questions, letters to their children, and prayer.

The goals for the studies are to teach God's plan for each individual as godly men, women, and parents, show them how to follow Christ and grow in their faith by developing godly habits, and to provide practical, biblical advice for life, marriage, and parenting.

Malachi Dads and *Hannah's Gift* graduates then attend Returning Hearts Celebrations. The inmates are not inmates that day. They are fathers and mothers who spend the day learning to share the love of Christ with their children while we take pictures of them together as a family. For many children, the first time they play a game or throw the ball around the yard with their dad is during a Returning Hearts Celebration.

We have a guardian program where we honor those caring for the children in the parents' absence. We serve a nice meal with gifts. We share the gospel and stories of how well the men or the women are doing in the Bible studies. We also help them prepare for the purpose of a Returning Heart Celebration, the time when each parent will sit down with their child, confess their sins, seek forgiveness, and hopefully begin reconciliation.

Recently, I ate with a father and his grown son while they shared their story during a Returning Hearts Celebration. As I have seen many times, the grown son was not a visitor; he was in prison with his dad.

The very young son had watched his father leave the house, never to return. He grew up feeling abandoned, angry, hurt, and bitter. Sadly, the son also had a young son of his own when he was sentenced to the same prison as his father.

Each of them signed up for the *Malachi Dads* Bible study, not knowing the other had also signed up, and by the providence of God, they were placed in the same small group of seven men. The father had come to faith several years prior. The son gave his heart to Christ by lesson six of *Malachi Dads*, and he immediately began to forgive his father.

Now, father and son walk around the yard together in prayer for the young boy struggling with anger and abandonment as he grows up without a father or grandfather. These three generations of men, all struggling with generational crime, are believing in faith that someday there will be full forgiveness and restoration by the power of God's Word.

Another wonderful restoration story came from the first *Hannah's Gift* graduating class. We wanted to honor Dr. Kristi Miller Anderson before the prison officials and female inmates, so we presented her with a plaque depicting the cover of her book. We had a beautiful ceremony where I spoke and the women gave testimonies celebrating what God was doing through *Hannah's Gift*.

At the end of the service, we invited the women to come to faith. One of the women came forward accompanied by another young lady who was especially emotional. Kristi knew both of them, so she prayed and cried with the young lady until long after the service was over. Most people were mingling, but I stood a few feet off to the side to be available in case I could help.

When they finished crying and praying, Kristi invited me to meet Hannah, the new sister in Christ, at the inaugural graduating class of *Hannah's Gift*. That day, the *Hannah's Gift* curriculum was born, and Hannah was born again through the mentoring of another inmate.

These are just two of the amazing stories that have come out of *Malachi Dads* and *Hannah's Gift* Bible studies and

Returning Hearts Celebrations. But this is only possible by God's grace and willing servants.

Lifeline Global is blessed with a small but powerful staff, including part-time workers who put in full-time hours and full-time staff who volunteer overtime. We have thousands of volunteers who teach *Malachi Dads* and *Hannah's Gift* and help run Returning Heart Celebrations. We could not do this ministry without our amazing staff and the many wonderful volunteers from around the world.

Be more concerned with your character than your reputation, because your character is what you really are, while your reputation is merely what others think you are.
—JOHN WOODEN

5
BUILDING HEALTHY FAMILIES FROM INSIDE PRISON

Get rid of all bitterness, rage and anger, brawling and slander, along with every form of malice. Be kind and compassionate to one another, forgiving each other, just as in Christ God forgave you.
—EPHESIANS 4:31-32

I heard a miraculous story of forgiveness one afternoon following the baptism of two men during a *Malachi Dads* graduation. After the ceremony, I met the men to welcome them to God's family and to hear their story. They both stood a few feet in front of me as they told me they were from rival gangs. Then, one man pointed to the other and said, "I killed his brother."

I stood before them speechless as the other man said he had completely forgiven his brother's killer. In fact, despite that the two men face threats from their previous gangs, they share the same cell, hang out together, and attend the same church services and Bible studies.

I share this story to illustrate how God can restore and heal relationships in the most tragic circumstances. To those of you who suffer from deep brokenness and years of separation, anger, and bitterness towards one another, I encourage you to know God is greater than any tragedy.

The Bible says to "get rid of all bitterness, rage and anger, brawling and slander, along with every form of malice" (Ephesians 4:31). This verse gives us a beautiful example of how Christ calls us to forgive one another because He has forgiven us. He can restore us if we come to Him for grace and strength. I invite you to bring your brokenness to the Lord, just as Christ came to us in brokenness. Go in humility and seek forgiveness, especially within your own family.

Most of our curriculum is about forgiveness and restoration. In fact, we have a whole book called *Family Restoration* used in both the men's and the women's Bible studies. Throughout the studies and discussions, we stress to begin restoration urgently. We advise the first step is to write their child a letter to ask for forgiveness in summary, without going into detail. Forgiveness is never an easy topic, but our experience tells us that most children are able to forgive their parents.

We find a lot of contrasts and misunderstandings among inmates about the concept of family. Sometimes the men and women in our programs think the government created the institutions of marriage and family for the benefit of society. They are surprised to learn that God designed people to live in relationships and to love and be loved in our marriages and families.

Many inmates did not have godly parents, so they don't understand how to be a parent or the impact they can have on their children's lives. We find this is especially common in men's prisons, where the inmates do not recognize their responsibility as a father. They have many children with a variety of mothers, and they don't know all their kids' names. However, most female inmates carry their children's pictures in the palm of their hand, and they burst into tears when asked about their children.

The foundation of our Bible studies is built on giving the inmates a godly concept of family and their roles as parents and spouses. We build that foundation through the core of our curricula expressed in the *Malachi Dads* and *Hannah's Gift* pledges. The pledges represent our philosophy of family, parenting, fatherhood, and motherhood in a few paragraphs.

We parent based upon who we are and what we've learned, especially from our parents. Most of the inmates grew up learning about crime rather than Christ, so the pledges of *Malachi Dads* and *Hannah's Gift* focus on growing as believers in Jesus Christ, beginning with what it means to be a godly father or mother.

To equip them to live it out in their families and communities, participants memorize the pledge and recite it at the start of each lesson. The pledges teach students to depend on God for strength and wisdom through Scripture and prayer so they can care for the gifts God has given them in their children.

MALACHI DADS PLEDGE

As a Malachi Dad, I solemnly pledge to glorify God and build His kingdom by prioritizing the raising of godly children, first in my family, then in the influencing of other men to do the same in theirs. I firmly believe that my transformed life in Christ—my life of integrity, pursuit of this vision, and the pursuit of godly character—will allow me to impact my children, family, and others towards this end.

I will practice a life of daily discipline and dependence on God through prayer and the study of God's Word for the wisdom in how to nurture my children in the admonition of the Lord. I will pursue this endeavor for a lifetime whether my children are in my home or not.

Finally, I believe that my end goal is not only for my children to walk in the Lord but this God-given vision would impact multiple generations to come, so help me God.

HANNAH'S GIFT PLEDGE

As a *Hannah's Gift* mom, I acknowledge that my children are a gift from God. I take hold of the call and responsibility as a mother, and I seek God's guidance on how to best parent my child. I am growing into a wise and strong woman of faith, and my greatest desire is to leave behind a spiritual legacy carried on by my children to their children. May my family prove to be a tower of strength built on the firm foundation I am laying in the power of Christ.

As inmates learn about the gift and responsibility of parenthood, we encourage them to write to their children, call them, and ask them to visit. Understandably, many loving, protective caregivers do not want to allow letters through or expose the child to prison. However, I would encourage guardians to consider the possible benefit of eye-to-eye contact between the wounded child and a restorative parent.

We encourage inmates to be both respectful and persistent because building family relationships can't wait until the last few months of a sentence. It may be years before the inmate is released, so restoration should be the priority from the first day. I have seen many inmates have beautiful, healthy relationships with their children from inside prison, even more so than some families I see at churches.

There are no easy solutions, but we offer a few practical suggestions to help inmates restore relationships from the inside and when they are released.

USE TECHNOLOGY

Technology improves every day. Take advantage of the tools available. Look for creative ways to reach out and maintain communication.

READ SCRIPTURE TOGETHER

Make a covenant to read the Bible together, and talk about it over the phone, virtually, or through letters.

DISCUSS GOD'S SOLUTIONS

Center your discussions on God's solutions and connect through the Bible. Talk less about problems and more about God's perspective on the issues.

VIDEOS

Find out if a local ministry comes into prisons to take videos of inmates to deliver to their families. Record yourself reading a story to your child so they can play it before bedtime. Encourage them and build them up so they will feel a little closer to you.

BIRTHDAY CARDS

Get birthday and Christmas gifts and cards through the canteen. Find out if you can send money to the guardians to buy a gift for the child from you.

MENTOR WITH OTHER INMATES

Mentor with or to another inmate, staff member, or volunteer to share ideas to help mend the relationship.

GET THE BOOKS

Family members can get the *Hannah's Gift* or *Malachi Dads* books online and do the Bible study with their loved one on the inside. By going over the material at the same time, the family members will understand what the inmate is learning, which leads to meaningful conversation and healing for everyone.

If the inmate is not in a facility we serve yet, we encourage family members to buy the books and guide their loved one through the study. In some communities, we have chaplains who will go to the family's home to help build those relationships.

LIVE FOR JESUS

The greatest thing you can do for your child is to live for Christ every day through your interactions with your child, other inmates, and officers. Ask God for opportunities to share your faith stories or other good things, but don't just preach to your children. Live more than you talk.

BE PATIENT

Both inside prison and when you are released, be patient in the process. Everyone has to adjust and learn to just be present again. Be patient with yourself, your children, your family, and your community.

Ask the Lord to give you a godly mentor on the outside to walk you through the process of reconnecting with your family, especially the first six months to a year after you go home.

NEVER GIVE UP

It's so easy to want to give up, especially during a long-term sentence. It's easy for the inmate to want to give up if the child is not allowed or willing to respond. I encourage both sides to please keep praying, writing, and calling, even if it seems like a closed door. Part of family restoration is a sense of endurance that only God can give, especially when you want to give up.

FAMILY FROM INSIDE PRISON

I have seen wonderful family relationships restored and evolve from persistence, endurance, and creativity, even when the inmate will never get out. Here is a very special story about just one of many godly relationships from inside prison.

Randy wanted to make things right with his family. He had a daughter he met briefly before he was incarcerated, but Ashley was too young to remember her father. Randy wrote to Ashley regularly and invited her to every Returning Hearts Celebration. Understandably, the girl's mother withheld the letters, but Randy didn't give up.

He wanted to be a responsible, godly father even if he never got out of prison. Randy kept writing, and after ten years, the mother allowed Ashley to read her father's letters. Through continued letters and phone calls, and by the graciousness and forgiveness of the mother, Randy became a real dad to his little girl for the first time.

Finally, Ashley met her daddy during a Returning Hearts Celebration when she was about ten years old. From then on, she came to Returning Hearts every year. Ashley came to Angola to see her dad every two months for many years, and they established a beautiful relationship.

Randy was very musical, so when he heard there was an old rusty piano inside the prison, he asked Warden Cain if he could have it. Warden Cain brought the piano inside and gave Randy the privilege of working on it. Randy made eleven guitars out of that throwaway piano, and then he sold them to send Ashley to summer Bible camp. Randy really was a father to his daughter, and Ashley was a daughter to her daddy.

During our Returning Hearts events, we set aside time for the inmates and children to reconcile. Toward the end of the event, we gather all the inmates and their families to sing and celebrate. Ashley was musically gifted, just like her daddy, so one year, when she was about thirteen, we asked them to sing for us. That day, Randy and his little girl sang the most beautiful hymns for two thousand inmates, children, and staff.

Every year, I looked for Randy and Ashley at the Returning Hearts Celebration. I would see them walking around, holding hands, not doing much of anything except just being a father and daughter for a day. I would say hello and ask how they were doing. Every year, I asked them to sing just for me, and they would sing "Amazing Grace" in the most heavenly harmony.

As she got older, Randy gave Ashley counsel about boys and dating, just like any other dad.

Returning Hearts is for children, so when Ashley was seventeen, she told me she would continue coming as a volunteer so she could see her dad.

As an adult, Ashley continues to share a beautiful relationship with her dad. Even though he will probably die in prison, Randy has a positive spiritual and fatherly influence over his beautiful daughter.

One day, God willing, I pray Randy will be released. But even if he isn't, they are still united as a family. Randy and Ashley's story is just one of many that illustrates the power of God's Word and how He uses Returning Hearts celebrations to reunite families and impact the next generation.

*Teaching that impacts is not head to head,
but heart to heart.*
—HOWARD G. HENDRICKS

PART 2
LESSONS FROM
PRISON MINISTRY

6
WHAT I HAVE LEARNED FROM THE INMATES

So God created mankind in his own image, in the image of God he created them; male and female he created them.
—GENESIS 1:27

When we think about inmates, it's typically an unpleasant thought laced with concern and fear. Some of us have personal hurt and brokenness because of an inmate's sin against us or our loved ones.

I felt this way for most of my life, but early in my prison ministry, Warden Burl Cain at Louisiana State Penitentiary taught me something I've never forgotten.

All men and women are made in the image of God; therefore, they have worth and value despite their terrible behavior. We need to see every inmate as though God sent

His only Son to save just them. As Christians, we must ask God to help us mirror the love of the Father to widows, families, *and* prisoners (Psalm 68:5).

I have been in more than seventy prisons around the world. When I see inmates today, the Lord helps me to see beyond their crimes to acknowledge the potential for what they can become if they follow Christ. For fifteen years, I have seen inmates serve as an instrument of restoration and forgiveness to their families in beautiful ways.

I have learned a lot from wonderful instructors, teachers, and professors from the time I was a boy through my doctoral work. I have known many inmates sentenced to ten years or more, so there is definitely brokenness, but in my mind and heart, the best teachers about walking with Christ are inmates, or as we like to call them, "returning citizens."

I want to share some of the things I've learned from returning citizens around the world over the last fifteen years.

PASSION FOR LEARNING

I have taught in churches, colleges, and prisons across America and around the world. My best students are inmates because they have a passion for learning. I have only seen such a passion to learn about God in prisons.

When many of my *Malachi Dads* and *Hannah's Gift* students were children, school had no value. Most of them had either abusive or negligent fathers, and their mothers had to work two or three jobs. As children, their lives were about survival, so they went to school to fill a chair, not to learn. Like me, a lot of the men and women either never completed high school or they got a GED.

But as I work with them, they're becoming transformed in Christ. They're hungry to learn, especially about God, the Bible, and about being a father or a mother. Many of our students read at a fourth-grade level, so they will look up words they don't understand and ask good questions.

HUMILITY AND BROKENNESS

The second thing I've learned is what it means to be broken before the Lord and other people. When you talk to a man or woman on the inside, there's a sense of humility I don't see elsewhere. They struggle with guilt, especially related to their families, their spouse, or their kids. Some of their struggles with guilt may be misplaced, and other times, it's appropriate, but there's a beautiful brokenness before God that we lack in our society today.

Often, we think we know it all. We have many degrees in education and successes in life, but we are all sinners. In God's eyes, we are just as broken as the inmates. We just don't admit it because of a big word we don't like to use in our society called *pride*.

As students feel safe in the small Bible study groups, I begin to hear their stories of brokenness before their God and other people. I've seen great, big middle-aged men get on their knees before their school-age children and ask for forgiveness. Perhaps the only thing more beautiful is the child's immediate forgiveness. Children are often the most forgiving people around.

One of the privileges I had was to visit death row at Angola. It was a new, high-tech facility with seven security checks. My wife and four other people accompanied me, so there were six of us in total.

We arrived at death row around 10 a.m. We walked down a long hallway. It was summer in Louisiana, and there was a fan but no air conditioning. On the left was a wall with televisions for the fourteen men in the cells on the right side of the hallway. Most of the men were still resting or sleeping, so we quietly prayer-walked past about seven cells until we saw a man who was awake.

I greeted him, and he was open to having a conversation. He asked why we were there. I told him we were there to do a Returning Hearts event the following day so inmates could have a carnival with their children to have fun eating and playing together, along with a spiritual time to bring hope and healing. He really liked the idea. He thought it was beautiful that the men could be together with their children for a day.

His home consisted of a bed, toilet, sink, and small table. On the table was a worn and tattered Bible. He spent his whole life in that cell, except for one hour each day to shower and exercise.

He was very warm and friendly. He told us a little bit about his family and where they were from. I asked him about the Bible. He said it was his favorite book, and he read it constantly because it gave him life and hope every day. I told him it's a wonderful book and to keep reading and learning about the Lord Jesus Christ.

Then it was time for us to go. I felt urged by the Spirit of God to ask him if he would mind if I prayed for him. He said that would be wonderful. I stuck my hand through the bar and took his hand. He was a muscle-bound man, probably in his forties, and he could have ripped my arm right off or killed me. But I felt led to reach out to him. I wanted to pray for him.

We all gathered near this man we just met as he allowed me the privilege of praying for him and his family. When I said, "Amen," he continued to hold my hand and started to pray the most beautiful prayer. He prayed for each of us by name and thanked God for us.

This broken man had such a unique, powerful, and intimate relationship with the Lord. He knew he would die in prison, yet it was overwhelming to see how God could use him to minister to us through such a genuine prayer. To hear a man on death row cry out for my soul and my life was life changing, as it was for the rest of my group.

We walked out of death row through the security checks and into the open area where the assistant warden of death row happened to be standing. I introduced myself and told her who I spoke with. I shared that we had a very positive conversation and told her about the Bible that looked very beaten up. I asked if I could bring the man a new Bible the next time I came, and she said that would be wonderful.

I bought him a really nice study Bible, but I did not get back to death row for about a year and a half. By then, he had moved to a different cell. I told the guard who I came to see, and he said I had two minutes. I was disappointed to have traveled so far to have such a short time, but I prayed to minister to the man as much as possible. The inmate was all the way at the end, and the guard was right behind me as I walked past every cell, so if I looked at anyone or said anything, he was there.

When we reached the last cell, the man recognized me. We greeted each other, and I said I was sorry it took so long. He was so grateful when I gave him the new Bible, and he said something very significant. He asked, "Why in the world would you buy this beautiful Bible for me and come all the way from California to give it to me?" His tone indicated he felt he had no value.

The guard was listening, and I knew my words had to be short. I looked at the gentleman and said, "I care about you because Christ died for you. You are made in the image of God. Because God sees you with worth and value, I see you with worth and value as a fellow human being, despite the circumstances we find ourselves in. God loves you, and I care about you. And I believe you can become a man of God even where you're at."

He looked at me and whispered, "I can't hardly believe that." That was about two minutes, and the guard tapped me on the shoulder and said, "Time's up." I said goodbye, and that was the last time I saw him.

The Bible says, "The Lord is close to the brokenhearted and saves those who are crushed in spirit" (Psalm 34:18). I have seen the intimacy between a broken inmate and his Savior, and I'm thankful I got to meet a man who genuinely loved God and His Word despite the circumstances of life.

There's a specialness in the broken people we have the honor of caring for. It's a beautiful thing I want to achieve someday.

HONESTY AND RESPONSIBILITY

The third thing I've learned from inmates is about truth. Most of us associate inmates with deception, but as they come to faith in Christ, they are brutally honest about their failures, especially regarding their families.

Many inmates have lived lives of deceit and dishonesty, which has impacted their children and their families more than anyone else. Sometimes, they say they don't think God can forgive them for all the bad things they have done.

It's a beautiful surprise to see an inmate display such raw honesty, perhaps for the first time in their life. When their heart is open to the Lord and to people willing to minister to them, we can help walk them through difficult conversations. As they continue to grow and mature in their faith, this translates into repairing trust with their children, their spouse, and their families.

As I have watched inmates learn to be honest with themselves and their loved ones, I have also learned what it means to take responsibility for our behavior, sin, and misconduct.

TENACITY

The men and women in our Bible studies do not give up on their children. They have tenacity in following through to make things right like I've never seen. Their endurance has taught me to persist when I don't get a reply from people. We all have challenges and get discouraged, but we can learn from their example of healthy endurance.

HOW TO MAKE UP FOR LOST TIME

Inmates have taught me to make up for lost time with their kids. After years of separation, the men and women constantly, persistently, and joyfully pursue ways to be present in their children's lives.

The beautiful thing about inmates is that once they see an open door to forgiveness and restoration, they don't go halfway. They go all in, and they don't let anything stop them from making up for lost time with their families and children.

We all have seasons of our lives when we've struggled, and we wish we could take them back. We can't recover the past, but forgiveness and restoration with a loved one can make a difference in the future, especially if we give all of our energy, strength, and heart to build the relationship.

The next time you see or hear a story about prisoners, I encourage you to remember Genesis 1:27, which says all men and women are made in the image of God. Of course, they need to pay their debt to society. I would not advocate that they should all be released, but we need to see them through a different lens.

If you struggle to get past fear or hurt regarding inmates, I pray the Lord may change your heart as He's changed mine so you can see their value, worth, and potential as God's creation.

We are all faced with a series of great opportunities brilliantly disguised as impossible situations.
—CHARLES R. SWINDOLL

7
WHAT I HAVE LEARNED FROM PRISON LEADERS

Now the overseer is to be above reproach, faithful to his wife, temperate, self-controlled, respectable, hospitable, able to teach.
1 TIMOTHY 3:2

I have had the opportunity to visit approximately seventy prisons worldwide. No facility is perfect, but I have met many outstanding leaders within the prison system. Despite mounting obstacles, these dedicated professionals work tirelessly to be an influence for good in moral rehabilitation.

As of this writing in 2023, there is a staffing crisis causing a cascade of unique issues. Many facilities are staffed at only 40 percent, so officers must work overtime dealing with inmates' challenging behaviors and mental health issues.[1] Sadly, wardens are forced to limit church services and other programming because there are not enough staff.

That tells you the strength of the officers that work diligently to make the prison safe for family members to visit. Over the last few years, society has raised the bar of appreciation for those who serve our community. I pray that attitudes of honor and respect extend to those who work in the front lines of our correctional facilities.

In this chapter, I'd like to honor two inspiring leaders who have spent their careers ministering to returning citizens around the world.

My experience in prison ministry began with a visit to Louisiana State Penitentiary in Angola, where I met Warden Burl Cain. Mr. Cain's career began as a high school teacher. During his first year, Burl told the school principal the job was too difficult, so he left to work in a prison! According to Burl, inmates are easier to work with than high school students. He served as warden of the Dixon Correctional Institute for fourteen years before he was invited to come to Angola in 1995.

Most wardens at Angola lasted four or five years because it was known as a violent, hopeless place where the worst criminals were sentenced to life in prison with no chance of

---

1   Drew Friedman, "New 25% retention bonuses at Bureau of Prisons only a 'Band-Aid' for larger staffing issues," Federal News Network, October 4, 2023, https://federalnewsnetwork.com/pay/2023/10/new-25-retention-bonuses-at-bureau-of-prisons-only-a-band-aid-for-larger-staffing-issues/.

parole. When Mr. Cain was approached to serve as warden, he made a counteroffer he thought they would never accept. Not long after, he became the very hesitant warden of the bloodiest prison in America.

Warden Cain was a Christian who sincerely wanted to make Angola a better place for both the officers and inmates, but he soon became so overwhelmed that he would cry out to God for help. As part of his duties, he was obligated to carry out death sentences. The first execution came early in his tenure. He was so torn that he barely said a word to the man as he methodically carried out the procedure.

Afterward, he confided in his mother that he didn't think he could continue as the warden of Angola, but she suggested that God had placed him in this position of leadership. She believed her son was called to influence the inmates to come to faith in Christ, especially the men on death row.

From then on, whenever Warden Cain was required to carry out a death sentence, he held the man's hand, talked with him, told him the good news of the gospel, and prayed for him. As Warden Cain ministered to inmates throughout the prison, he came to see every man as a human being made in the image of God with the potential to change and be transformed.

Warden Cain wanted to bring reform and peace to Angola. He recognized that God was the only one who could heal such brokenness, so he coined the phrase *moral rehabilitation* to explain spiritual things to a secular audience. Everyone wants society to be moral, so the phrase served as a bridge to begin communication with state and federal officials who would help him reform the prison.

Warden Cain has received the Warden of the Year Award, the Distinguished Service Award, the National Leadership Award, and others, as God used him all to implement moral rehabilitation in prisons around the world.

He believed the most important path to prison reform was through the transformation of the men and women inside. He was an educator at heart, so one of his first initiatives was to establish a fully accredited Bible college inside Angola with the help of the New Orleans Baptist Theological Seminary (NOBTS). Seminary professors volunteered their time and expertise, driving two and a half hours to teach the inmates using donated seminary texts. These amazing ministers received no compensation. They did it out of compassion for the men and in service to God. Thanks to their outpouring of love, life inmates earned a four-year ministry degree with an emphasis in counseling.

At that time, there were eight prisons in Louisiana. As the men graduated from Bible college, they would visit other prisons in groups of four or five men to help the chaplains start *Malachi Dads*, *Hannah's Gift*, and other Bible studies. Most of the men came to Angola before they were twenty-one years old, and the average sentence was ninety-three years, so the seminary students were trained to be leaders and pastors. As more men earned seminary degrees and attended Bible studies, they began to ask Warden Cain if they could hold church services inside the prison. At the time of this writing, there are over two dozen churches inside Angola, all pastored by long-term or lifer inmates.

Burl Cain privately funded six chapels, all built by inmates, so God would be honored throughout the prison, and moral rehabilitation would be the norm. Toward the end of his career, inmates worked in eight-hour shifts around the clock to build a chapel to seat three hundred people. Thanks to the dedication of the inmates, the chapel was completed in thirty-nine days.

One of the great leadership principles of Burl Cain is that he saw men who did the worst of the worst with dignity because they are made in the image of God. Despite their crimes, he cared about each man. Of course, there are consequences for disruptive behavior, but he still treated the men with dignity, honor, and respect in every way he could.

Another leadership principle was to keep the men busy working, using their talents and gifts. Angola had been a huge financial burden on the state of Louisiana, but Warden Cain almost turned Angola into a self-sustaining city, complete with its own zip code.

Unless a man was a safety risk or had physical limitations, every inmate had a job inside prison. He had a reason to get up in the morning and contribute. The men were productive eight hours a day, so they were tired and less likely to cause trouble in the evening. The men were also paid a small wage so they could send the money to their families or spend it at the canteen.

Louisiana State Penitentiary is on 18,000 acres of farmland, so Warden Cain put it to use. The inmates grow much of their own food instead of relying on state funds. Other inmates tend farm animals or train police dogs and horses. They also maintain the state vehicles.

Men serving life sentences with no chance of parole will die of old age and other natural causes, so Warden Cain created the first prison hospice center where fellow inmates are trained to care for their dying brothers. When an inmate passes, his friends will escort a horse-drawn carriage, singing hymns and songs, to his final resting place in one of seven campus cemeteries, all maintained by inmate sextons.

Unfortunately, several men fell out of their cardboard boxes on the way to the cemetery, so Warden Cain constructed a woodshop where talented men could build beautiful caskets. By this, everyone knew that Burl Cain cared about the dignity and value of every man, in both life and death.

Warden Cain also organized fun activities for the inmates. Not all the men got to participate due to bad behavior, but those who did, enjoyed it, and it produced better behavior. For example, he organized sporting leagues, including a baseball team called "Malachi Dads."

They even built a professional quality rodeo, which is still held there today. I've been to the rodeo, and it was outstanding. Men with good behavior can train for the rodeo and participate in front of an audience for the community. The prison charges admission to raise funds for the seminary and other fun activities.

Warden Cain had the most simple and effective way of earning the inmates' trust and respect. I remember walking with him down the hallways by the cells, and the inmates would give him a piece of paper, a note scratched out in pencil or pen. Burl put them in his pocket until we got back to his office. Then he took all those pieces of paper and read the needs or concerns the men expressed. He either personally responded to each one, or, if necessary, delegated to a relevant staff member.

The same thing happened when he attended church with the men or anywhere else he walked around the prison. Every inmate knew he had access to the warden and that they would get a reply. This simple system earned Warden Cain incredible trust, respect, and credibility among the men, even when he had to discipline disruptive behavior.

Mr. Burl Cain was used by God to bring hope and restoration to the men inside Angola for twenty-one years.

When he became warden, a life sentence meant the man would never be free, but laws are changing.

There were forty men in the first *Malachi Dads* graduating class. At the time of this writing, about twenty-five of the men have been released. Most of them are doing well in their jobs, churches, family relationships, and marriages. I have met former Angola inmates who now work for their sentencing judge as mentors for young men going through the judicial system.

The Bible college that started approximately forty-five years ago is now in twenty-one states, all training men to be spiritual leaders and assisting chaplains to bring the good news of Christ to many who are incarcerated.

An educator who became a warden, Burl Cain is still working very hard at age eighty as Commissioner of the Mississippi Department of Corrections. All of this and so much more happened under Warden Burl Cain's leadership.

I also want to tell you about Chief Alex Yim. He was a hardened cop who preferred to work alone, even in the most challenging neighborhoods. He loved arresting criminals and "throwing the keys away" to let them suffer the consequences of their behavior. Alex loved being a cop and making the neighborhoods safe, so he worked his way up the ranks to become chief of police for the largest jail system in America, the Los Angeles (L.A.) County Jail.

As he moved up in rank and authority, Alex also matured in his faith with the help of his pastor son, Brent. During a visit to Angola Prison, Alex learned that, while the inmates had to accept the responsibility of their crimes, they still had value and potential as men made in the image of God. As chief of police, Alex always honored his responsibility to fulfill the law, but God used Brent to help his dad see the men for what they could become.

Sadly, Brent died in his early thirties, leaving behind a wife and two young children. While this was traumatic for the whole family, God used all that pain and grief to continue to shape Alex into a man of strength and compassion.

Chief Yim held many special events to recognize men who earned their GED or other achievements. I will never forget a graduation ceremony I attended one hot summer afternoon. There were about one hundred fifty inmates and fifty lawyers, councilmen, and city officials in attendance. The event could not begin until Chief Yim and the sheriff arrived, and they were a few minutes late that day. When they arrived and walked onto the platform, the inmates gave them a standing ovation to honor them for all they were doing in Los Angeles County.

It seemed like such an oxymoron; I was just blown away. These men were in jail, some of them for several years, because of officers and leaders of the sheriff's department, so the standing ovation was a beautiful gesture of honor and respect.

Like Warden Cain, Chief Yim had a system to be accessible and to hear from the inmates so they would know he cared. Chief Yim would invite up to two hundred men to a meeting where he would sit with them and hear their questions and concerns. He was always as transparent as he could be. If it was inappropriate for him to answer a question, he would be honest about that, too.

What caught my attention most was the way Alex spoke to the men with respect, and how the inmates responded in kind. The men appreciated Chief Yim's time, but they were more impacted by how he treated them. He even shared personal tidbits occasionally. I was there the day he shared his family's grief at the loss of his son, Brent. The inmates responded with compassion and love. It was one of the most beautiful scenes I've ever witnessed in a prison or jail setting. Like Warden Cain, Chief Yim was respected by the inmates because he was both tough and tender.

Alex Yim retired after thirty years as a police officer and started teaching *Malachi Dads* in a state prison. When he told his first class what he did for a living, a few of the men got up and walked out. But he went on caring for and teaching the rest of the class, along with hundreds of other men, in the next few years. In fact, at one time, there were over 150 men enrolled in *Malachi Dads* because of Alex Yim's leadership. After Alex retired from teaching *Malachi Dads*, a wonderful, godly man he mentored took over, so *Malachi Dads* is still going strong.

These two men provided excellent, godly leadership in the most difficult circumstances. With Burl Cain, God used a hesitant educator to teach thousands of men the good news of the gospel. With Alex Yim, God used a hardened cop who became a man who honored both the law and the dignity of those who broke it.

As you think about the men and women who work in our jails and prisons, know that some of the greatest leaders in America have dedicated their lives to keeping everyone inside safe. They have a challenging job, but it can also be a transformational experience. So, if you meet someone who works in a correctional facility, please acknowledge them to honor their sacrifice.

Success is not final, failure is not fatal: it is the courage to continue that counts.
—WINSTON CHURCHILL

PART 3
THE FUTURE OF PRISON MINISTRY

8
INTERNATIONAL PRISONS . . . GO

He said to them, "Go into all the world and preach the gospel to all creation."
—MARK 16:15

My interview for the role of director of Lifeline Global was with Jack Eggar, the president of Awana Clubs International. A visionary by nature, Jack had big plans for the future of Lifeline Global. He commented that it was strange for Awana Clubs to be in 120 nations in the world, while Lifeline Global was only in the United States. Jack wanted to take Lifeline Global internationally. At that time, we were in about five prisons through five states, so we were still a new ministry.

I probably should not have interrupted the president of the company in the middle of an interview, but that's what I did. I told him we have about 2.3 million inmates in the United States, and I didn't think I had time to go to other countries. He didn't hear a word I said. He just kept on talking about how we were going to take this ministry beyond US borders.

Somehow, I got the job, and soon after that, I met with my friend Frank, a lead chaplain from Los Angeles County jails. He wanted Lifeline Global to be part of his new ministry in the Dominican Republic. Frank connected me with Brian Berman, prison warden and president of Project Mañana, a prison reform program in the Dominican Republic. I still felt out of my element, but when they mentioned tacos, I figured I had nothing to lose in meeting him. So, I had a nice lunch, made a new friend in ministry, and forever altered the future of Lifeline Global.

DOMINICAN REPUBLIC

Over lunch, Brian invited my wife and me to visit him to learn about Project Mañana. Frank even offered to sponsor our flight through his ministry, Only Hope. I had never been to the Dominican Republic, and I figured it would be interesting to see what prisons were like there, so I accepted his generous offer.

I had no experience in international ministries, but Brian is a skilled leader. We prayed and planned alongside his team and other key leaders. By the grace of God, we brought *Malachi Dads* into the Dominican Republic under the banner of Project Mañana in 2013. We began with small steps, but after a few years, I knew I needed someone to help me with the international ministry. The man I fondly refer to as "the best hire I ever made" is our international director, Dan Bostrum.

Dan grew up on an international mission field and then moved to the United States to attend college. He got married and spent thirty years in a career in education. Dan's missionary heart was always there, so during his career and after, he and his wife took short-term mission projects around the world whenever they could, including volunteer work at Returning Hearts Celebrations.

I got to know Dan as we traveled home by car from a Returning Hearts Celebration in Illinois. I saw that he was really a missionary disguised as a teacher. I saw his passion for international ministries, his missionary heart expressed through his teaching skills. The team at Lifeline Global was just starting work in the Dominican Republic, and as I listened to his story, I felt the prompting of the Lord to ask him to join us as our unpaid international director. Much to my surprise, he didn't care that I couldn't pay him because the Lord had blessed him with a good pension. He took the position and raised funds through his church to cover travel expenses.

Dan's first job was to help me with the Dominican Republic. When we started, the only prison guards were located outside, surrounding the buildings, so the inmates could not escape. Inside, the inmates lived their personal and professional lives.

Brian, Frank, and I befriended key leaders in the Dominican prison system. They even came to Angola to learn about Returning Hearts Celebrations from Warden Burl Cain. Warden Cain helped us work through security issues alongside Brian Berman.

One of the leaders was skeptical about bringing *Malachi Dads* into Dominican prisons, so he attended a Bible study to learn more. Participants had to seek forgiveness from a family member, and the prison leader had a severely fractured relationship with his mother. He procrastinated as long as possible, but eventually wrote to his mother. His mother responded with forgiveness and reconciliation. They are a beautiful model of love, forgiveness, and grace.

That was the beginning of his journey of becoming a Christ follower. As he learned from the Bible, he took both his faith and his job seriously. As a key leader, he had the authority and influence to implement change aligned with biblical principles. Every day the security guards and forty

Malachi Dads graduates meet for prayer. They discuss any broken relationships among the inmates so peace can be restored. The meeting is closed in prayer before anyone goes to bed. They do not let the sun go down on their anger.

As of 2023, *Malachi Dads* and *Hannah's Gift* are in fifteen of the twenty prisons in the Dominican Republic as part of Project Mañana, the new model of award-winning prison reform led by Brian Berman. Through Project Mañana under Brian's leadership, there is appropriate discipline, education, and Bible studies. The Project Mañana leadership refers to *Malachi Dads* and *Hannah's Gift* as "authentic manhood/womanhood." In fact, every aspiring security guard in the Dominican prison system has to go through the *Malachi Dads* Bible study before they can work there.

Thanks to Project Mañana, the guards and inmates pray together, and peace is more prevalent. Every year, a Returning Hearts Celebration is held at one of the Project Mañana prisons. For one day, the men and women are not inmates. They are fathers and mothers seeking hope, healing, and restoration with their children.

Crime is down inside Dominican prisons, and conditions are much better for both inmates and officers. We are so honored and humbled to be a part of Project Mañana and other similar efforts around the world where we get to help inmates become godly men, women, fathers, and mothers in their own language.

CUBA

When Cuban borders began to open during President Obama's administration, ministry partners Bob and Carol Collins asked if we wanted to start *Malachi Dads* and *Hannah's Gift* in Cuban prisons. We worked through Mr. Collin's mission organization to get through the political red tape and gain permission to train approximately seventy-five chaplains.

My wife and I flew to Cuba with six other people to stay in the home of a very generous and gracious host. At that time, the average family of four in Cuba lived on twenty dollars per month. He hosted all eight of us, fed us, introduced us to his family, and taught us how to work in the Cuban culture.

Our first training was on the east coast of Cuba, about one hundred miles away, and we had to pick up many of the chaplains on our way. The Lord gave us skilled translators, women who traveled around the country with us through the muggy, subterranean climate in a van with no air conditioning on roads that had not been maintained in sixty years.

We stopped at a pastor's home that also served as a church for around thirty or so people. Gas stations were few, so we took a little break with every opportunity to top off the tank and use the restroom before the gas station offered us coffee we could barely stir.

Ten hours later, we arrived at the church. The little chapel had hard chairs and no windows or air conditioning. With the help of our translators, we trained approximately seventy-five chaplains, who were beautiful Christian brothers and sisters.

When we got done with the conference, our host and other people from various parts of Cuba took us to a river a few miles from the church. We jumped in with all our clothes on to cool off from the heat. When we got out of the water, our hosts walked us a little way down the river where a few chaplains tended to two beautifully roasted pigs. Given the economic conditions, I will never understand how they did it, but they prepared a lovely celebration for us.

We learned that over half of their community of 70,000 people were Christians, in comparison to 5–10 percent in our hometown in Santa Clarita, California. We were just amazed at the power of the gospel. The Cuban chaplains were so excited about the gospel and being able to share it in prisons that it was cause for an elaborate celebration. It was one of the most beautiful experiences of my life.

The second training was as amazing as the first. Early in the conference, a few chaplains announced they wanted to publish *Malachi Dads* and *Hannah's Gift* and have them printed right in Cuba. I was stunned. Most of the chaplains couldn't afford a Bible and had never held a Bible study in their hands. The crowd was so excited they gave the chaplains a standing ovation.

Later, during the second training, the chaplains decided to pray over a prison being built in the community and for the future inmates. Sadly, they were not allowed, but that didn't stop them. They worked out a plan to take shifts walking around the prison in prayer between 10:00 p.m. and 2:00 a.m. for six weeks.

We did many other trainings during our stay in Cuba. During every training, a pastor and his family would invite us to their home for a meal. Most homes were about four hundred square feet, so we filled the entire house. The women usually prepared rice and beans. Occasionally, they would throw in a little chicken.

We began to understand the poverty early in our trip, so each of the wives in our group would give the lady of the house twenty dollars at every visit; every family that hosted us received between $80–$100. We knew this was several months' salary for them, but we were grateful for their selfless generosity and graciousness.

As we prepared to go back to the United States, Debbie and I discussed the future of using *Malachi Dads* and *Hannah's Gift* in Cuba. I asked our leader how much it would cost to translate and print per book. He said it would be about a dollar and a quarter per book. I knew I couldn't match that price in the United States, not to mention the shipping costs and the challenges of getting the materials to the right people. Next, I asked our leader how many books we would need. He said we needed about 8,000 books to take *Malachi Dads* and *Hannah's Gift* into prisons all over Cuba.

Our team was thrilled at the prospect of being able to touch the lives of prisoners and their families in Cuba with the good news of restoration in their own language. But all I could think of at that moment, besides being hot, was that if my math was correct, it would cost approximately $10,000. My wife and I have been married for over fifty years, so she knew exactly what I was thinking.

I told the group that I didn't know how I could get that much money. They didn't hear the word *money*. They only heard the words *spread the gospel*. They were not going to be stopped, but they were not responsible for raising the money. It was up to me. Amid this discussion, I cried out to God and said, "Yes, Lord, I'm going to go home by faith and try to see what You are going to do!"

Five days after we got back, I received a note in the mail from a woman. Debbie and I were close to the woman and her husband. They had supported Lifeline Global until the husband passed away two years prior. The note said one of her husband's CDs came due for $10,000, and she didn't need the money. She knew her husband loved what we were doing, and she thought we could use the money.

She didn't know I had been to Cuba or that we needed $10,000 to get these Bible studies into the hands of many inmates and families. As I read her note and held the check in my hands, I cried and thanked God for the generosity of this woman. I called her to tell her the story, and we had a nice cry together over the good hand of God being upon us.

But He still was not done. With money in hand, we moved forward with the search for a translator. One of the translators during our trip was a young Cuban college graduate in her twenties. Dan Bostrum and I both noticed her translation skills and exceptional fluency in English, so I asked her about translating *Malachi Dads* and *Hannah's Gift*. She was interested, so we gave her six pages of another Lifeline Global curriculum. We gave her sample to the translation department of Awana Clubs International in Chicago, where professional translators served around 120 countries. The experts in Chicago loved her work so much they wanted to hire her.

Dan and I were sold. We gave our young lady friend in Cuba three of our books to translate from English to Spanish. Sometimes the computer connection was poor, but she pushed through it. She wanted to do the work as a gift to Lifeline Global; however, Dan and I understood the economic situation in Cuba. We knew she represented the hearts of many Christians we met who want to serve Christ no matter the cost. She did a beautiful job translating all three books to Spanish, and she deserved payment for her work.

When you live and travel together, you get to know one another. The Cuban chaplains and our translators had something we sometimes lack in the United States. They had tenacity. We can learn so much about real, sacrificial ministry from our brothers and sisters in Christ.

The Cubans are beautiful people. I still maintain contact with some of the people I met. At Lifeline Global, we support our Cuban partners in Christ as much as we can, and it always warms my heart to get their letters telling of dozens of prisoners coming to Christ through *Malachi Dads* and *Hannah's Gift*.

I have told you about just two countries that model the others we serve. Now, thanks to Dan's leadership, the Lifeline Global ministry is blessed to be in some of the most difficult prisons throughout twenty countries in Africa, Europe, Central America, and the Caribbean, and our curricula are translated into fifteen languages.

Jack Eggar, my friend and former president of Awana, was right. My vision was limited. I have repented of my attitude and lack of vision to take the good news in the prisons and the other countries. I thank God for Dan Bostrum, who God raised to help Lifeline Global bring *Malachi Dads* and *Hannah's Gift* to more than twenty countries around the world.

Here is a list of countries with Lifeline Global International Ministries:

Belarus	New Zealand
Burundi	Nigeria
Cameroon	Romania
Costa Rica	Russia
Cuba	Rwanda
Dominican Republic	Sierra Leone
Ghana	South Africa
India	Tanzania
Kenya	Uganda
Kyrgyzstan	Ukraine
Lithuania	Zambia
Malawi	Zimbabwe
Moldova	

Don't you have a saying, "It's still four months until harvest"? I tell you, open your eyes and look at the fields! They are ripe for harvest.
—JOHN 4:35

9
HOW CHURCHES CAN GET INVOLVED IN PRISON MINISTRY

Then Jesus came to them and said, "All authority in heaven and on earth has been given to me. Therefore go and make disciples of all nations, baptizing them in the name of the Father and of the Son and of the Holy Spirit."
—MATTHEW 28:18-19

Instead of the word *inmate* or *ex-con*, we need to refer to people leaving prison as *returning citizens*. They have lived the consequences of their mistakes, so we need to view them through a mindset that gives them a chance to start over.

I have pastored in eight different churches around the United States over my fifty-three years in ministry. For my first twenty years as a pastor, I drove past L.A. County jails every day and I looked the other way. In 2007, I had to confess my sins to my Lord and repent of ignoring His basic command to care for prisoners the same way we care for children, widows, and orphans. It was transformational once I got involved in prison ministry.

Now, when I speak at churches, I face the same apathy I had. I have spoken at churches where people stood up in the middle of my talk, insisted that criminals deserve to rot in jail, and marched out of the room. Other times, church members and leaders agree the Bible says we should care for the prisoners, but then we never hear from them again.

I understand people feel uncomfortable with the idea of visiting prisons, but Christ calls us to serve the lowly and broken. The apathy of the church is heartbreaking for me and my staff, but God helps us to be patient because He is also patient with us.

We are thankful for the churches and the individuals who have supported Lifeline Global and other prison ministries with their time, talent, prayer, and resources. Prison Ministry is complicated and political. Many times, it is three steps forward and two steps back, but the experience always changes the staff and the men and women inside.

Our mission goes beyond the inmates to serve their families, their children, and even their unborn grandchildren. Lifeline Global exists to break the generational cycle of incarceration, so we speak to their hearts' sometimes secret desire for a godly relationship with their children. We are asking God to break the cycle, to change the family for the next 100 years. It's an overwhelming challenge, but there is nothing more beautiful than to witness God's forgiveness and healing in the men, women, and families we serve.

In October 2023, PrisonPolicy.org reported that around 2 million Americans are incarcerated, and 2.6 million children have parents in jail or prison.[2] God is bigger than the sins of crime and apathy, so I believe these statistics represent a great potential for Him to mobilize the church for a spiritual revival through our returning citizens.

In the book of Acts, Saul persecuted the church until Jesus rescued him from sin and selfishness. Jesus changed Saul's name to Paul, and He used him as one of the greatest leaders in the church's history.

I'm praying for the body of Christ to minister to our Sauls who will become Pauls. As a pastor for over fifty years, I know the church has the greatest army in the world for Jesus Christ. He will raise up a leader who will make a difference in even the most difficult places.

HOW TO SERVE IN PRISON MINISTRY

So, what practical steps can the body of Christ take to be part of this mission? There are thousands of beautiful prison ministries out there. Ministries such as Prison Fellowship

---

[2] Emily Widra, "Ten statistics about the scale and impact of mass incarceration in the U.S.," Prison Policy Initiative, October 24, 2023, https://www.prisonpolicy.org/blog/2023/10/24/ten-statistics/.

are in all fifty states and many countries around the world. Others are small neighborhood ministries where one chaplain serves one or two prisons. Whether you are alone or one of thousands, there are many ways to minister to our returning citizens.

PRAY

The first thing you can do is pray for both the men and women inside and those who serve them. Research to learn about prison ministries and get the name of an inmate or prison worker to pray over them specifically.

ATTEND SERVICE

Consider reaching out to a local warden or prison ministry to learn how you can serve. One of the most impactful things you can do is attend a prison chapel service or volunteer with a chaplain.

Some of the most memorable church services I've ever attended were in prison. For instance, I once went to a chapel baptismal service led by a godly chaplain in a prison on the coast of California. The chaplain asked each of the twenty men to testify briefly before baptizing them in the name of the Father, Son, and Holy Spirit. When they came out of the water, a community leader dressed in a beautiful suit hugged each dripping-wet man to celebrate their decision to follow

Christ as the congregation praised the Lord for the new believer's step of obedience in being baptized.

Friends, you have to be very hard-hearted not to be moved. I encourage you to attend chapel services or volunteer with chaplains or prison ministries so you can meet some of these men and women on the inside.

REFLECT ON THE VISIT

After your visit, don't continue with your day as though this was just another appointment. Reflect on what God is teaching you about serving the broken people in your community. We can all be used by God to play a little part in reaching out to those in jails and prisons.

VISIT WITH YOUR CHURCH LEADERS

Visit with your pastors, elders, deacons, and other church leaders to get the congregation involved. Psalm 78:1–4 is important to us at Lifeline Global because it motivates us to pass on God's truth to incarcerated parents and their children through our program.

Just like local churches, the staff at Lifeline Global is a family ministry, so we share Psalm 78 and other passages to inspire them to get involved with equipping and training fathers and mothers to be godly parents. We encourage them to impact the next generation even if they don't get involved with Lifeline.

My people, hear my teaching;
listen to the words of my mouth.
I will open my mouth with a parable;
I will utter hidden things, things from of old—
things we have heard and known,
things our ancestors have told us.
We will not hide them from their descendants;
we will tell the next generation
the praiseworthy deeds of the LORD,
his power, and the wonders he has done.
—PSALM 78:1-4

MOBILIZE VOLUNTEERS

Whether on your own or in partnership with your church, contact a local prison leader to find out how you can mobilize volunteers to be a part of prison ministries. There are men and women interested in prison ministry in every church. In my experience, the first people to step forward usually seem to have some rough edges. They come from difficult backgrounds that may include past incarceration. They may not fit in well with the children's ministry, but they have a passionate faith in Christ. They may look a little tough, but they've been serving the Lord for ten or twenty years and searching for a clear ministry.

In my experience, these people are the best prison workers because they understand the returning citizens' struggles. They can see past the crime to connect with the hurt. When they meet the heart of the returning citizen where they are, they can lead them to Christ.

As a volunteer, you think you are going to minister to the inmates, but in reality, most volunteers tell me they receive much more than they could ever give. Many volunteers find their kingdom calling and purpose inside prisons.

RAISE RESOURCES

Raise resources and funds to pay for prison ministries. Prison ministries struggle to raise funds and resources because inmates are not well-regarded in our society. Most of them are serving the consequences of their behavior, but they still have value, worth, and a voice.

Prison ministry is a mission ministry. People give money to missions all over the world, as we should. I would just challenge you to consider generosity toward prison-related ministries.

One of the most beautiful prison ministries is the Gideons, which gives out thousands of Bibles every year all over the world. I would encourage you or your church to see if your local jail or prison needs Bibles to minister to the inmates directly. I recommend the New International Version (NIV) because it is easier to read and understand. Call the facility beforehand because wardens or chaplains must approve any item that comes inside the prison.

At Lifeline Global, it is always a challenge to raise enough money for our books. Most cost only five dollars each, but thousands of men and women all over the world are waiting.

JOIN LIFELINE GLOBAL

Join Lifeline Global by teaching *Malachi Dads* or *Hannah's Gift* or help with a Returning Hearts Celebration event.

Some of our volunteers have overcome their own trauma by serving in prison ministry. For example, one woman struggled with the trauma of witnessing her dad's arrest in the middle of the night when she was a little girl. Despite her fears, she still wanted to serve in prison ministry and went through training with us. However, she was too nervous to come in with us during our first visit to L.A. County jail.

The following year, she returned with grace, strength, and courage. She worked past her trauma and fears and came with a beautiful smile. As she met with the inmates and their children, God brought healing and victory to her heart.

I remember another volunteer, a business owner, who got special permission to share how he had found Christ and forgiveness with the inmates in the same prison where he had served time ten years prior. Despite the risk, he was determined to tell the men how thankful he was for what

Christ had done to change him. Now, he hires returning citizens, and he generously supports Lifeline Global.

I'm so proud of people who overcome challenging circumstances. Come see and be a part of someone's journey to becoming a beautiful new creature in Christ. If you have an open heart, you will also be impacted by the transformation of these men and women from Sauls to Pauls.

The heart of service and generosity through prison ministry is summed up beautifully in Ephesians 2:10, which says, "For we are God's handiwork, created in Christ Jesus to do good works, which God prepared in advance for us to do." If you are a disciple of Jesus Christ, I challenge you through Scriptures such as Hebrews 13:3; Psalm 78:1–4; Ephesians 2:10, and many others to get involved with prison ministries.

We are grateful for the many volunteers who have served with Lifeline Global. Safety is always our priority, and we have had no incidents of physical or emotional conflict. In fact, in closing this chapter I would say it's safer to go to prison with me than it is to go to the mall.

My email address is at the end of the book. Please contact me, and I will be glad to share ways to get involved. Come and join me. Let's go to prison together.

God has marvelous ways of taking our worst tragedies and turning them into His most glorious triumphs.
—JOSEPH STOWELL

10
FINISHING WELL

> *And the things you have heard me say in the presence of many witnesses entrust to reliable people who will also be qualified to teach others.*
> —2 TIMOTHY 2:2

At the time of this writing, I am seventy-five years old. My time as the full-time director of Lifeline Global may be limited, but I'm grateful for the years I spent serving in prison ministry. It's been life-changing, and I want to finish well for the families we serve and the glory of God.

While I never had to raise money as a church pastor, fundraising is the most intimidating and challenging part of my work as a missionary. I want to thank God for kicking me out of my comfort zone to learn to trust Him for the resources we need.

The hardest parts of my job take place outside prison walls. Every day, the greatest challenge is convincing fellow believers to be generous to those behind bars. We may think they don't deserve a second chance, but in God's economy, we all get second, third, fourth, fifth chances or more.

I thank God for those who quietly and faithfully pray for Lifeline Global Ministries. I am also grateful for those who give generously to our calling. I believe being generous is part of finishing well. God asks us to continue to learn to be generous, even in the last years of our lives. We need to have our hands and pocketbooks open to see what God will do to transform and restore families.

As I transitioned from a church family pastor into prison ministry, I was so motivated as I saw the transformation of ungodly men growing more like Christ. It's a special gift to watch a man open the Bible for the first time. In jails and prisons, it's normal to see the Sauls of the world joyfully transformed into Pauls with a passion for Christ.

I met many inmates with strong yet misdirected leadership skills. Gangs are part of the culture in many jails, so inmates who come to faith while in jail have an even greater impact for good.

And yet that passion to share the Word and bring hope and healing to others was a very rare sight in the safety of a local church. During my years as a church pastor, I learned that men's ministry has many challenges, obstacles, and opportunities. I feel like I failed to equip and disciple men in the church to be the spiritual leaders of their homes, churches, businesses, and communities.

But it is not too late, even at my age. You may expect I am thinking about retirement, counting down the days until I can spend my last years on vacation. A life of leisure is the goal for most people; however, the concept of a relaxing retirement is not in the Bible.

The Bible does not define retirement as a life of leisure to begin at a certain age. My goal is to finish well and continue to grow in Christ in my family life, personal life, and ministry.

Please understand, I'm not against relaxation or vacations. In fact, the Bible tells us to rest one day every week, but God calls us to serve Him and grow more like Christ for all of our life. Scripture repeatedly tells us to continue walking in our calling until our last breath. We are called to finish well.

The Old Testament includes a great example of finishing well. In Numbers 13–14, we find the story of the Israelite men Joshua sent to explore the Promised Land. When the men returned from their expedition, all but Joshua and Caleb said the people were too powerful to overcome, and the land was not inhabitable. As word spread through the camp, the Israelites did their normal routine; they complained and whined that it would have been better to die as slaves in Egypt.

That is, everyone except Joshua and Caleb.

> *Joshua son of Nun and Caleb son of Jephunneh, who were among those who had explored the land, tore their clothes and said to the entire Israelite assembly, "The land we passed through and explored is exceedingly good. If the LORD is pleased with us, he will lead us into that land, a land flowing with milk and honey, and will give it to us. Only do not rebel against the LORD. And do not be afraid of the people of the land, because we will devour them. Their protection is gone, but the LORD is with us. Do not be afraid of them."*
> NUMBERS 14:6-9

The people didn't listen. Instead, they contemplated stoning Caleb, who was forty years old at the time. The Lord God became angry with their continued complaining and disobedience, so none of the nation lived to see the Promised Land—except Joshua and Caleb.

> *"Not one of them will ever see the land I promised on oath to their ancestors. No one who has treated me with contempt will ever see it. But because my servant Caleb has a different spirit and follows me*

wholeheartedly, I will bring him into the land he went to, and his descendants will inherit it."

NUMBERS 14:23-24

For the next forty-five years, Caleb continued to serve God faithfully, and he indeed came into the Promised Land. In the book of Joshua, we meet Caleb again. At the age of eighty-five, he is ready for a new assignment from the Lord.

"Now then, just as the LORD promised, he has kept me alive for forty-five years since the time he said this to Moses, while Israel moved about in the wilderness. So here I am today, eighty-five years old! I am still as strong today as the day Moses sent me out; I'm just as vigorous to go out to battle now as I was then. Now give me this hill country that the LORD promised me that day. You yourself heard then that the Anakites were there and their cities were large and fortified, but, the LORD helping me, I will drive them out just as he said" (Joshua 14:10–12).

Joshua and Caleb were called to step out and trust God, even in the face of opposition. They heard the fears and complaints of their people, but they listened to God rather than men. Joshua and Caleb did not complain to God even though their task felt overwhelming on their own.

Hebrews 11:6 says, "And without faith it is impossible to please God because anyone who comes to him must believe that he exists and that he rewards those who earnestly seek him." Raising resources for ministry is definitely a step of faith, and as a prison ministry, some people would rather tell us to leave than consider what we have to say. Prison ministers and all believers must seek God through his Word so we can endure opposition and finish well. That might mean taking a risk or doing something out of the norm for a believer of your generation.

We want to end well, whether it's in prison ministry or another ministry the Lord has called us to. Mature believers need to focus on finishing well for the glory of God, the good of our families, and the influence of our community.

My life's greatest delight and fulfillment is pointing inmates and their families to the cross through *Malachi Dads* and *Hannah's Gift*. Lifeline Global and the men and women in prisons have motivated and influenced me to conclude my life well and to be a better man of God.

I don't know what your calling could be or should be, but perhaps there is more to life than planning vacations and spending thousands of dollars on leisure. Caleb is a beautiful example of how we can follow God's plans for us to invest well in the later stages of life.

I encourage you more mature believers out there to ask our heavenly Father how to spend your retirement years. Listen to church and ministry leaders and consider how you may have the passion and skills to contribute. Pray for clarity to see the needs around you and seek direction to serve during the last years of your life.

You can retire from your vocation, but you can never retire from your calling.
—TODD SMITH

Being a role model is the most powerful form of educating. Youngsters need good models more than they need critics. It's one of a parent's greatest responsibilities and opportunities.
—JOHN WOODEN

11
A NEW MODEL FOR PRISONS

For we are God's handiwork, created in Christ Jesus to do good works, which God prepared in advance for us to do.
—EPHESIANS 2:10

I become a student of every prison I visit. I observe and learn from what is happening with the inmates and staff, especially from a spiritual and relational standpoint. I am not an expert in things such as security protocol or gang relationships, but I have learned a lot about what makes for a successful spiritual dynamic inside prisons. I have also observed that every other part of the man functions better when his spirit is at peace.

Over 95 percent of the inmates in America will eventually be released back into society. No one wants to go back to jail, but sadly, approximately half of them will return within just three years.[3] Prisons of the future need to consider how to equip inmates for life outside prison. Incarceration is intended to be disciplinary, as it should be, but it should also be rehabilitative. Punishment without learning is a disservice to both the inmates and society.

A new model for prison will give inmates the tools they need to make good decisions, earn a living, raise capable children, and contribute to society. In most facilities, reentry strategies begin a few months before the inmate is released, but that is not enough. We need to start preparing for reentry on their first day behind bars.

Every facility is a little different, but I'm convinced educational opportunities must be part of a new model for prisons in the future. Facilities that invest in the education of the inmates have a much better culture. Many inmates do not have a high school diploma, a GED, or proficient reading and writing skills. I applaud prisons and jails that offer GED programs, but prison leaders need to partner with educational institutions to give inmates the life and job skills they need.

I encourage you to think about strategies for the inmates to get back into society as productive citizens with a meaningful life ahead of them. Here are a few successful

---

3   "Reentry Fact Sheet," US Department of Justice, https://www.justice.gov/sites/default/files/usao-ndga/legacy/2014/12/12/Reentry%20Fact%20Sheet%20_FINAL.pdf.

programs we can look to as models for both secular and spiritual opportunities:

SECULAR EDUCATION

Throughout this book, we have focused on spiritual growth and healing for the inmate and the prison but, of course, most Christians do not spend their careers in ministry. While I am not an expert in secular education, I have seen trusted inmates lead productive lives as a result of learning a skill inside prison through community colleges, local businesses, and peer mentoring.

COMMUNITY COLLEGES

Prison leaders can partner with community colleges to provide options for vocational training. Providing education to inmates gives community colleges the opportunity to increase their student enrollment and revenue and fulfill their mission to make education available to all local residents. By collaborating with community colleges, prisons can strengthen and expand their educational services to prepare inmates more effectively for their transition to life beyond prison.

LOCAL BUSINESSES

Another vital area to improve the prison atmosphere is to recruit community businesses to do certified training for the county or state, such as teaching inmates to repair state-owned vehicles. They can also earn certificates in other trades, for instance, HVAC. Whether they use the skill to work in the prison, to teach other inmates, or to get a job upon release, it's a benefit to the inmate, the prison, and the community.

PEER MENTORING

We must move past the fear of peer-to-peer mentoring inside prisons because an inmate who has gone through a spiritual or vocational certification program needs to be a role model and an inspiration to others. Mentoring gives the mentor a purpose in being part of another inmate's reentry strategy while the student gains new skills.

Those who have gone through a biblical curriculum will influence their peers spiritually to bring about true change and healing to each other and the prison atmosphere. Godly men and women within the prison can be used by God to transform a lifestyle of warfare and conflict to a culture of peace and harmony.

SPIRITUAL EDUCATION

There is a movement of the Lord through biblical curriculum used inside prisons around the world. Prisons offering seminary training have a beautiful, God-honoring culture focused on spiritual growth and mutual respect for both officers and inmates. This kind of environment helps inmates mature, learn more effective coping strategies, and build healthier relationships both in prison and when they reunite with their families.

Many repeat offenders try to start a new life upon their release, but they do not have the skills, guidance, or protection to overcome the influence of their previous street gang. However, I have seen many inmates renounce their gangs through the spiritual education and support available both inside prison and upon release.

When a former gang leader applies their skills to ministry, they are a mighty force of God. We have seen God transform lives of crime into lives for Christ through spiritual programming with the Urban Ministry Institute, the New Orleans Baptist Theological Seminary, and Lifeline Global.

THE URBAN MINISTRY INSTITUTION

The Urban Ministry Institution (TUMI) is an outstanding curriculum run by World Impact. They provide a three-year diploma including nonaccredited Bible ministry classes that teach men and women to be spiritual leaders in prison or when they get out. The curriculum is challenging and developed so well that some Christian colleges accept transfer credits from TUMI.

NOBTS PRISON SEMINARY FOUNDATION (PSF)

Under Burl Cain's leadership, the PSF offers four-year, fully accredited degrees for inmates in Bible, ministry, and counseling. The PSF is now in twenty-one states training the next generation of Christian leaders in prisons and in our communities. That, my friends, is true moral rehabilitation.

LIFELINE CURRICULUM

Upon release, most inmates and their families need to mend the relationships while also adjusting to a new routine and family dynamic. Even when the loved one's release is welcomed and celebrated, so much change is stressful for everyone. But if relationships are strained, then families are divided, and assimilation into family life is exponentially harder.

Many inmates did not have or observe healthy relationships growing up. They never learned how to be a spouse or a parent or how to resolve hurt and conflict. Through *Malachi Dads* and *Hannah's Gift*, students begin to build healthy family relationships while they are still inside, so the transition following release will be smoother.

As of this writing, Lifeline Global is at work in thirty-three states and growing. While Lifeline Global is not part of NOBTS, we have prospered and grown wherever NOBTS is already at work. NOBTS graduates are eager to teach

Malachi Dads and *Hannah's Gift*, and they are some of the most inspiring and impactful facilitators.

Facilitators teach relational skills within the context of reentering the family. For example, the inmates learn the value of writing to their children to celebrate their birthdays, holidays, and special events. They also learn about forgiveness, communication, and how God teaches us to love one another.

CONCLUSION

I have seen returning citizens stand up for Christ in difficult places, so I believe men and women inside prisons can be the next spiritual revival in America. I'm praying for a movement of God through inmates who are now transformed from darkness to light and ready to shine in their communities and churches.

The catalyst must be prison leaders like Warden Burl Cain and Chief Alex Yim, who can think creatively within prison protocol and inmate safety. Prison leaders of the future must be willing to endure scrutiny, secure in their goals to improve life for officers and inmates inside, and prepare men and women for successful reentry into the community.

Through *Malachi Dads* and *Hannah's Gift*, we are committed to that mission. We're thankful we can have a small part in prisons in America and around the world to bring hope and to bring families together again.

Our hope is in Christ. Our mission at Lifeline Global is to restore and equip incarcerated men and women to become godly parents, so that the generational cycle of incarceration can be broken.

WILL YOU JOIN ME?

I have not failed. I've just found 10,000 ways that won't work.

—THOMAS A. EDISON

KEY BIBLE VERSES FOR THE INMATE IN ALL OF US

JOHN 3:16
For God so loved the world that he gave his one and only Son, that whoever believes in him shall not perish but have eternal life.

ROMANS 3:23
For all have sinned and fall short of the glory of God.

ROMANS 6:23
For the wages of sin is death, but the gift of God is eternal life in Christ Jesus our Lord.

ROMANS 10:9-10
If you declare with your mouth, "Jesus is Lord," and believe in your heart that God raised him from the dead, you will be saved. For it is with your heart that you believe and are

justified, and it is with your mouth that you profess your faith and are saved.

MALACHI 4:6

He will turn the hearts of the parents to their children, and the hearts of the children to their parents; or else I will come and strike the land with total destruction.

1 SAMUEL 1:28

"So now I give him to the LORD. For his whole life he will be given over to the LORD." And he worshiped the LORD there.

HEBREWS 13:3

Continue to remember those in prison as if you were together with them in prison, and those who are mistreated as if you yourselves were suffering.

GENESIS 1:27

So God created mankind in his own image, in the image of God he created them; male and female he created them.

PSALM 34:17-18

The righteous cry out, and the LORD hears them; he delivers them from all their troubles. The LORD is close to the brokenhearted and saves those who are crushed in spirit.

PRAYER OF SALVATION

Dear God in heaven, I come to You in the name of Jesus. I acknowledge to You that I am a sinner, and I am sorry for my sins and the life I've lived. I need Your forgiveness. I believe that Your only begotten Son, Jesus Christ, shed His precious blood on the cross and died for my sins.

You say in Your Holy Word, in Romans 10:9, if we confess that Jesus Christ is our Lord and believe in our hearts You raised Him from the dead, we shall be saved. Right now, I confess that Jesus Christ is my Savior. With my heart, I believe You raised Him from the dead. This very moment, I accept Jesus Christ as my Lord and Savior and surrender to Him. According to Your Word, right now, I am saved.

I thank You, Jesus, for Your abundant grace, which has saved me from judgment for my sins. I thank You, Jesus, that Your grace never leads to more sin but rather always leads to repentance. Therefore, Lord Jesus, transform my life so I may bring glory and honor to You alone and not to myself.

Thank You for dying for me and giving me eternal life. Amen.

Name: _____
Date: _____

LIFELINE GLOBAL CURRICULUM

CURRICULUM

We have created a suite of products to help you on your journey of knowing and applying master truths. Visit our website lifelineglobal.org and click on the CURRICULUM CENTER for full details on how to order.

Malachi Dads™
The Heart of a Father

This 12-week curriculum for men's prison ministry provides practical biblical advice for life, marriage and parenting.
Available in Spanish

Malachi Dads™
The Heart of a Father Six-Week Study

This new six-week curriculum is designed for men's prison and jail ministries and provides practical biblical advice for life, marriage and parenting shows men how to take steps towards reconciliation.

Malachi Dads™
The Heart of a Man - Part 1

Show incarcerated fathers how they can have a heart that pleases God, regardless of their past sins. This study includes 12 lessons and facilitator's notes.
Available in Spanish

Malachi Dads™
The Heart of a Man - Part 2

Includes lessons designed to help men live as godly examples in their families and communities. This curriculum for men's prison ministry provides practical, biblical advice for life, marriage and parenting.
Available in Spanish

Malachi Dads™
Family Restoration

This book gives incarcerated fathers biblical steps for building healthy relationships with their families. It includes 10 lessons, along with facilitator's notes.
Available in Spanish

Malachi Dads™ Psalm One

This 5-week Bible study (introductory to Malachi Dads™) was written by inmates who are godly men and leaders of Malachi Dads at Louisiana State Penitentiary at Angola.
Available in Spanish

Hannah's Gift™
The Heart of a Mother

A 10-week program especially for women's prison ministry. Modeled after the life of Hannah and her son as told in the Old Testament, this curriculum offers mothers the opportunity to parent from a distance and give a legacy of faith to their children. Also available as a six-week study. *Ten-week study available in Spanish*

Hannah's Gift™
Family Restoration

This book gives incarcerated mothers biblical steps for building healthy relationships with their families. It includes 10 lessons, along with facilitator's notes.
Available in Spanish

Hannah's Gift™
Beautiful Woman

Identifies key struggles that cause women to forfeit their happiness and joy. These 10 lessons are designed to help women find their place as beautiful woman in this world.

Hannah's Gift™ Psalm 23

Be encouraged and reminded that you are never alone with six brief lessons, based on Psalm 23 and written by Hannah's Gift participants.

Equip Leaders
Small Group Prison Ministry

This guide prepares Malachi Dads and Hannah's Gift facilitators to effectively lead inmate small groups. Each chapter includes key verses, biblical foundations, methods, teaching pointers and more.
Available in Spanish

Inmate Challenge Video

A compelling challenge from some of the most broken men in our society — inmate fathers. This video accompanies Lesson 11 in The Heart of a Father book and an optional seventh lesson in the six-week study. Running time: 25 minutes.

ABOUT THE AUTHOR

MIKE BROYLES has been a pastor for over fifty-three years and the Executive Director of Lifeline Global Ministries for over twelve years. He has a Bachelor of Religious Education from Grace University, a Master of Arts in Christian Education from Talbot School of Theology, and a Doctor of Religious Education from Temple Baptist Seminary.

Mike is blessed to have Debbie beside him for over fifty-two years. They have two sons, Dan and Jon, and two daughters-in-law, Carli and Jocelyn. They are most blessed with seven grandchildren: Emma, Nate, Josiah, Nolan, Lucas, Eli, and Saffron.